This is your Brain on Shamrocks 2:
50 Shades o' Green

MIKE FARRAGHER

CONTENTS

Foreward

1   Acknowledgements   9

2   What Is a Brain on Shamrocks?   12

3   An Auld Fella   15

4   Peas in a Pod   18

5   Irish Mammy Heroics   21

6   A Lenten Pizza Penance   23

7   Clouded Vision   25

8   Let's Toast the Pioneers!   28

9   What Will the Neighbors Think?   30

10 Remembering the Cross Woman   33

11 The Tough Man With the Soft Center   36

12 The Cross with the Prize Inside   38

13 Origins   40

14 A Name by Any Other Name   42

15 Judging the Wake   45

16 When I Was Your Age...   47

17 Have Mercy in the Parking Lot   51

18 Farewell to a Fashionista   53

19 Late Ain't Great   55

CONTENTS

20 Tom Jones and the "Commando Performance"   58

21 A "Destiny" with Teen Angst   60

22 How Did We Come to This?   62

23 Off Kilter   66

24 Dial 911 for a Zero   69

25 Too Fat for Toro   75

26 A Learned Eejit   79

27 Back to School is No Longer Tough   81

28 A Frank Discussion About Neighbors   84

29 Laughter is NOT the Best Medicine   86

30 Let's Dance!   88

31 Girly Man o' the Grid Iron   91

32 Comic Book Blues   93

33 What Is Irish?   96

34 The Jamaican Shamrock   98

35 Green Car in the Race to Nowhere   104

36 Remember Golden Deeds in Golden Years   107

37 High School Musical Love   110

38 Property Brothers for Sainthood   113

39 Confession App   116

CONTENTS

40	Clean Up Yer Act	118
41	Pray for My Wife	120
42	Screw U Haikus	122
43	Robbery at 20,000 Feet	126
44	Don't Mess with the Nuns	128
45	A "Tail" of Woe	131
46	Parting is Such Sweet Sorrow: Pogues Review	135
47	My Big Fat Gypsy Wedding Review	137
48	What Your Irish Music Says About You	140
49	Reading Into My Influences	143
50	How It All Began	149
51	A Write Pain	153
52	Write On!	157
53	Bonus Book: 50 Shades o'Green	163

Foreword

As editor of the *Irish Voice* newspaper, I get dozens of resumes from writers anxious to break into the business.

To this day, Mike Farragher's pitch stands out in my mind.

The year was 1997. The *Irish Voice* was looking for a new rock music correspondent, so we advertised a freelance position in the paper. The applicant had to have a deep knowledge of the Irish music scene and a willingness to review concerts, CDs and the like. No prior writing experience was necessary, but the candidate had to be able to express thoughts and opinions in a way that would make the reader want more each week.

So along comes Mike's resume in the snail mail. Resume isn't the right word, really–his pages-long pitch, wrapped in a neat plastic folder, opened with a large picture of himself wearing some sort of Irish T-shirt and, I believe, a tweed cap. There were also references to Guinness, shamrocks, shillelaghs–all the usual tacky, stereotypical stuff.

Ugh, I thought. *This dude's a weirdo.* The thought of him representing the *Irish Voice* out and about kind of filled me with dread and embarrassment.

But what is it they say…don't judge a book by its cover?

I thumbed through the rest of the package and I had to admit, his enthusiasm for all things Irish became infectious. Never had anyone come across so eager to be part of the *Irish Voice* team, and behold, the guy could actually write! A music writer and critic was born. Truth: Mike has blossomed into much more in the years since, as his burgeoning stable of books clearly shows.

Mike truly made his mark in the Irish-American music community as a respected observer who writes with sass and style. But there are only so many CDs and shows a writer can review. Sometimes, in slow weeks, Mike was finding it difficult to fill his "Off the Record" page in the *Irish Voice* with interesting copy.

A few years ago he approached me with an idea: to broaden his column to include his observations about family life, his experiences growing up as the child of Irish immigrants, raising two girls of his own with his Jewish wife—that sort of thing. He sent over a few samples, and I could relate to them on many levels. I felt sure that our readers would feel the same way.

Although we have very different musical tastes, Mike and I are alike in other ways. I too am the child of Irish immigrants, and though he's a Jersey boy and I'm a Long Island girl, our experiences growing up are quite similar.

My parents came to America with practically nothing, but were determined that the next generation–my brother and I—had all the opportunities they did not. Mike's parents raised him and his brother with exactly the same mindset.

Catholic school stories of horror and joy, shopping with Mom at Sears for extra-large clothing, spending summer holidays in Ireland…been there, done that, just like Mike. On occasion, Mike's column makes me laugh out loud. He's so incredibly honest about himself and what he sees as his shortcomings.

One column in particular that he wrote in 2010, "A Whiter Shade of Pale," became an instant classic in my mind. Mike described in hilarious detail a Farragher family day at a scorching hot beach—not the best place to be when your ethnic skin freaks out at the sight of the sun, and your bones and muscle are hidden under layers of "extra" flesh.

"The red-berry skin tags that dot my ribcage and the congealed white sunblock crusting around the nipples of my B-cup man-boobs add to the beach blanket fright-fest that is my disrobing," he wrote.

"As usual I deflect the uncomfortable situation with humor, which is why I usually wear a shirt that says either 'Winning the War Against Anorexia' or 'Preparing for Famine' that I bought in every color to coordinate with each bathing suit in my wardrobe."

Mike paints pictures with his words—the image that comes to mind in the aforementioned scene isn't as gruesome as he imagines because his body isn't as scary as he thinks!—and he does so with true passion and style.

He's extremely proud of his association with the *Irish Voice*, and the feeling is mutual. He's got a brain, all right—and it's filled not only with shamrocks but so much more, as his regular readers will attest.

It's been a real pleasure to watch Mike develop his own true Irish-American voice in the pages of our paper each week. He'll be doing so for a long time to come.

-Debbie Mcgoldrick, Senior Editor, Irish Voice, October 2012

Acknowledgments

This book is dedicated to Ann Cleary-Moynihan of Fargo, North Dakota, because a) she has believed in my writing ability when few did and b) she raised such holy hell that I didn't mention her in the first installment of *This Is Your Brain on Shamrocks,* I dare not write another book without giving her an 'auld mention!'

A funny thing happens at the holiday gathering right after you come out with a book of your family's stories—half the people in the clan are pissed off that you mentioned them in the book and the other half are pissed that you didn't! You can't win for losing!

My love for my family should have been pretty evident in the first installment, and I've grown to love them even more for their support during the never-ending book tour on both sides of the Atlantic. I can't thank Marie Forde enough for being the best unpaid publicist a cousin could ask for when I brought *Shamrocks* to Ireland. The book ignited conversations with some cousins that have deepened our relationship and I treasure them now more than ever. I even ran into bona-fide cousins I never knew I had!

When you write a book about a family with a wicked sense of humor, you find out pretty quickly who doesn't possess a sense of humor in the group. Hopefully you'll get the joke this time around, or you'll deny me three times before the cock crows like St. Peter did, once you read the accounts of sexual and pharmacological misadventures within these pages. However it goes, I love you anyway.

There wouldn't be a sequel if the first one didn't do decent business and I am clear that this happened because of many individuals and businesses. Thanks to Steve Jones and Dalmar James at Websignia for their digital imprint on the website and the strategies to take my words viral on the Internet; kudos to Kevin Adkins for the brilliant artwork because people *do* judge a book because of the cover; the staff of Fiddleheads Restaurant, St. Stephen's, Paddy Reilly's, Puck, and Boston's Four Green Fields, for their hospitality; to independent booksellers like Booktowne and Clinton Bookshop for publicizing a kindred independent spirit. Thanks to the musicians who brought stellar performances to the "rock and read" events on the *Shamrocks* book tour to include Thom and Deirdre of Beannacht, Seamus Kelleher, Celtic Cross, Seanchai and the Unity Squad, Joe Hurley, Jimmy Smith and Mighty Avon Radio, *The Tuam Herald*, Larry Kirwan, Sirius Satellite Radio's *Celtic Crush* program, and Black 47.

Thank you to Irish American Writers & Artists Inc., a group of creative souls who have provided inspiration and encouragement to voices like mine. I enjoy spirited creative dialogue with Jennifer Bruursema, Dalmar James, Jim Sanderson, Peggy Madden-Marano, Larry Kirwan, and Honor Molloy and their encouraging spirit was essential in the writing process.

I would also like to thank WFUV, Eileen Cronin of Long Ireland Radio, and especially Louanne Dunphy of Celtic Crossings on WMUA for her early belief in *Shamrocks*.

Debbie McGoldrick, Niall O'Dowd, and the staff at the *Irish Voice* and IrishCentral.com have been in my corner since Day One and there would be no "Mike Farragher the writer" without their initial belief in me when I was so, well, "green."

Most people think you have to master grammar to be a good writer and I tell those people that writers have no concern with that stuff. That's what editors do! Brian Blatz is the best in the business. He is my oldest and one of my closest friends and he has no idea how much I love him and value his opinion. Collaborating with him on each book just brings us closer together, an added bonus to this nonsense. A special shout-out to my good friend John Mitchell for his second set of eyes in the copyediting process!

Phil Duffy's photography makes me look studly and I think the Vatican should canonize him for creating such a miracle.

People ask me all the time: what did Mom and Dad think of the last book? Well, they are private people who, at first, weren't thrilled about the whole world knowing these family stories. They got over the rough language in some spots of the first book, got the true intention behind the book, and eventually joined the fun at most book signings. I love them and it tears my shit to pieces when I think of how the bad language I sometimes use bothers them. I will try to use cuss words sparingly this time around. Promise!

My wife, Barbara, and my daughters, Annie and Maura, are my universe. I love them and if I didn't *have* to dedicate the book to Ann, they would have been next in line. Honest.

OK, now all that's out of the way…let's go!

What Is a Brain on Shamrocks?

This is your brain on shamrocks:

Like most minds, your thought process is guided by that inner voice that judges and assesses everyone and everything. In fact, that voice might have just asked, *what voice is he talking about?*

Yup. It's *that* voice.

But you're an Irish-American born to Irish parents, which means your inner voice has a brogue that sounds remarkably like your mother's. It's that "Celtic consciousness" that gets to work as you're sitting on the back deck of your house reading the Sunday *New York Times* just as the last Mass of the day begins.

Not going to church this morning, are we? Well, I'm sure the Lord Jesus Christ didn't want to get up the day he died for yer sins! Yerra, I'm sure he would have had more fun doing the crossword puzzle instead of hanging on the cross!

On the motorcycle road trip of your life, that inner voice will be in the sidecar, offering color commentary on the scenery that whizzes by. If you find yourself putting the kickstand down in the parking lot of a tattoo parlor in your late forties, for example, that voice will encourage you to stick to the bright lights of the interstate.

Is there a church nearby? While you're in there marking up your arm so that it looks like a coloring book, I want to get a few decades of the rosary in. I will be praying to the Mother of God that ye'll come to your senses. Not sure what ye are tryin' to prove here. Are ye trying to set an example for my granddaughters? I'm sure they're gonna wanna run off and get one of them tramp stamps above their rumps. Sure, that'll be a marvelous look. But ye go ahead and do what ye want, luv. What do I know?

You try to argue with that voice but there is no winning. The voice always lands a guilt-punch below the belt and radiates pain throughout the body as you lay in a fetal position on the curb.

Nine pushes. 'Twas nine of the most agonizing pushes a mother ever had to suffer to give birth to a child and if I could have known that the son I gave birth to would talk to his mother's voice in his head like that, sure, I wouldn't have bothered pushing at all.

Everyone needs a vacation and your inner voice is no exception. When and if you are able to shut it off, a new voice that sounds remarkably like Sister Rita slides into the sidecar.

She was the servant of God who taught your sex-education course in the sixth grade. Like a rabbit under the shadow of a swooping hawk, you can remember how your breathing became labored as the woman you affectionately nicknamed "Fish Face" walked down the aisle of your classroom.

Her delight as she described Hell was palpable…the way the Earth periodically parted to burp out the stench of burning flesh, the cold gurgling sludge of eternal suffering, and the loss of the Lord's light. How you got your ticket punched for a one-way trip to eternal damnation was the favorite part of her lecture. Sister Rita's voice usually screeches in your ear whenever a hint of intimacy is in the air.

Violating your body with pleasures of the flesh is a mortal sin, especially when you are alone. A mortal sin produces a macula that stains the soul and if it is not immediately repented in Confession, you will be eternally separated from God in Hell. If you die and a mortal sin like premarital canoodling is not confessed and repented for at the time of your death, it will result in an internal and agonizing damnation!

You never thought you'd ever beg for your mother's voice to make an encore performance inside your skull, but Sister Rita can do that to you. Sister Rita and the inner voice are partners in the shaping of your life: the fear of eternal damnation and an Irish mother's guilt allow you to stay in the right lane of good behavior.

You were raised at a time and culture where parents and teachers never encouraged their children to be anything they wanted to be. The world was painted as just a big blue ball orbiting the sun, it was never positioned as your oyster! They paid enough for your education, but all that was expected of you was to not embarrass them in front of the neighbors. If you became a priest or nun, your parents would die with a smile on their face. But if all you did was manage by some miracle to scale a few rungs higher on the socioeconomic ladder, fair play to you.

Indeed, the inner voice may mock you once your income bracket rises. It's a cruel irony that your parents toiled in lower-middle-class drudgery so that you could get a college degree and then hire lower-middle-class people to do the menial jobs around the house that are no longer worth your time. Your head never gets as big as your bank accounts, thanks to that voice inside your head.

So, I guess we're all highfalutin' now, are we? Too good to clean your own house and mow your own lawn? Yes, I know ye'll tell yourself that ye have made enough money for ye to allow yer wife to stay home and raise the kids, and I'm glad for ye, luv. Really. Ye went a lot further in life than I ever thought ye would. But it wouldn't kill yeh to clean the auld toilet once in a while.

Your parents never spent money on maids and landscapers. They tended their own house and saved every penny they could to provide for you and send what little money was left to their own parents in Ireland. If overtime wages and tips were good on any given year, they may have taken you over to see your grandparents. Those childhood trips to Ballylanders and Athenry in the motherland are stitched into the fabric of your soul and Ireland calls you, her traveling child, to come home every few years.

The inner voice has a belly full of Irish pride on St. Patrick's Day, furious at the portrayal of our culture.

Do they all think we are all eejits swillin' green beer and puking our guts out along the parade route? Ye are handy with a pen—dash off a few words to the Hallmark Card Company and tell them that we'll burn a leprechaun card every day until they start printing greetings with St. Patrick instead of green beer!

You thought that voice was stark raving mad all these years, but now you won't hoist a pint before first stopping at church on March 17. It is there that you reflect on God's many blessings in your life. You married way above your station, your children are angels, your parents are in fine health into their later years, and you live in abundant love with your friends and family. You say a silent prayer to the saint who was captured and carried off as a slave to Ireland in his teens, asking him to watch over your economically battered homeland right before you light a candle and bow to your Maker.

I like the way you ended this, luv. Fair play to yeh. Maybe I didn't do such a bad job raising yeh after all.

This is your brain on shamrocks.

Book 1: *The Rearview Mirror*

One of the great things about writing this book, and the last one, is that you get to reflect and then share the colorful ways of characters that make up the fabric of your past. It's essential to keep these stories and memories alive—if we won't, who will?

An Auld Fella: A Contractor's Worst Nightmare

Despite living a safe distance from the coast, my friend Peggie bore the brunt of the Hurricane Irene when it lasered through the Garden State. Right after trees crashed onto her cars and house, the insurance company dispatched contractors to make the repairs. On one Saturday morning, her 89-year-old father, Mick Madden from Portumna County Galway, went to inspect the work of the Brazilian crew that buzzed around her property.

I'm told he shook his head in disgust as soon as he got out of the car.

"Ye nail two pieces of wood together in this country and they call him a carpenter."

This sounds a lot like my dad, who was born not far away from Madden in Athenry. He would always offer to "let the fellas in" while I was on the road and workers were doing something around my house. That would put him in the catbird seat to be the contracting equivalent of an *America's Got Talent* judge. He'd never be more than a few paces away from the work at hand, making sure we got what we paid for and more. "I didn't think anyone was more useless than you are with a wrench, but I stand corrected," he might say to me after a plumber left behind a shoddy job when I had supervised things.

Though they are too gentlemanly to boast, the fact is that guys like Mick Madden and my dad, Mick Farragher, ("No one was called 'Mike' over at home," Madden informed me) came from the lush farms of Ireland to either build this country and/or keep it running. Dad was a roofer for a while to keep the roof over our heads while Madden kept the lights on and everything humming as a superintendent of his Jersey City apartment building.

These 'auld fellas' are in their 70s and 80s now and they just don't build 'em like them anymore. They've forgotten more about common-sense approaches to broken things than most modern workers have ever learned and today's workers know it, which makes these old guys a contractor's nightmare.

God forbid a painter drips something on the carpet. The auld fella hovering nearby might suggest he places a rubber band around an open paint can to wipe your brush on—it keeps paint off the side of the can as well. On the rare event when this hopeless "narrowback" tried to build something, I might have been advised by my old fella that a simple pocket comb was the secret weapon to keep that wobbly nail in place before you laid a hammer onto one of your fingers.

My Uncle Tim is a sharp guy, master mason, and all-around handyman in his day. He could make something out of nothing; I remember how he would cut patterns from discarded plywood at a construction site he worked on, paint it white, and *voila*! You had life-size reindeer lawn ornaments that he sold by the truckload for a small fortune during the holidays.

He isn't short of opinions and is a bit of a loud talker, two weapons I have used to my advantage while I was shopping for houses a few years ago.

"Jaysis, did Stevie Wonder set this stone?" he might exclaim as he'd stare up the side of the brick facing on a potential house. "'Tis a miracle that it stayed up as long as it has. And don't get me started on the inside, with all those brown splotches on the ceiling. It tells me that there was a lot of water damage once—and yer man did a woeful job covering it up before he put it on the market, like."

When we would submit a low bid for the property, Uncle Tom's booming voice would echo in the heads of the real estate agents before any higher counterproposal was suggested.

They may label themselves as an uneducated lot because they left school at the tender age of 15, yet the "auld fellas" have smarts to burn that you just can't hire nowadays.

Peas in a Pod

When I walk the dogs, I often see a Peapod truck pull into the driveway of someone's home. The driver will hop out, lift the back door of the truck, dock a small metal ramp between the back of the truck and the driveway, and proceed to unload large green totes full of food.

Peapod is a service of Stop & Shop, a national grocery store chain. According to the website, busy moms on the go can hop online, select a grocery list by brand name, order their provisions, and log off. No bulky shopping carts! No little grabby hands at the checkout line chucking sweets onto the conveyor belt! No effort whatsoever!

The knuckle-dragging Neanderthal in me has a huge problem with this and I know some female readers are about to take issue with what I say next. It's one thing for a full-time working mother to avail herself of these services, but most of the customers of Peapod in my neck of the woods are women who don't work outside the home. What the heck makes their lives so busy that they can't hoof it up and down the aisles once a week to save their poor working husbands a few bob? This is so not the Irish way, I say smugly to myself.

History and an ancient memory tell me otherwise, however.

"Didn't the Irish invent that Peapod thing 60 years ago with the traveling cart?" my father sniffed dismissively when I shared the sighting of this truck a few doors down.

I remember well the traveling cart during visits to my parents' birthplace during summer vacations.

This portable shop was a lifeline to the many families on the outskirts of Tuam. My grandmother and my uncle who lived with her never owned a car, so the traveling cart was the only means to get groceries without pestering my uncle next door for a ride into town all the time.

A small truck would line up next to the razor-straight hedges that lined the front gate of Granny Farragher's house. In this neck of the woods, the man known as "Glynn from Corofin" would amble through the neighborhood selling his goods.

"Howeyeh, Missus?" Glynn would say, tipping the hat to her. He'd look down at me and my brother. "Who are these Yanks?"

"Mick's kids," she'd say proudly. "And aren't they as well-behaved as the man himself?"

"It would seem so," he'd say with a smile. "Real 'doteens'."

Granny would take off her thick bifocals, wiping the fingerprint smudges from them with her apron. She'd balance the eyeglasses on her thin nose, inspecting the brilliant oranges and dried fruit in wooden crates that were stacked on display cases in the back of a flatbed.

"Faith n' ye'll needn't make another stop on the rest of this road, what with all the visitors we have here and all the people coming around to see them. These Yanks have a grand appetite altogether."

The goods would be displayed on an angle that resembled the pitch on a roof. There would be one section that would be stocked with black pudding, sausages, salted ham, and butter. My brother and I would make our way to the other side of the truck, where he would display the Cadbury Aero bars, currant cake, apple pie, and sweet cake. We were taught never to interrupt adults while they were talking, especially if one of those adults was Granny Farragher, so we patiently waited for her to finish the order before we'd gamely ask her for a chocolate bar. The transaction took forever, as Glynn would playfully haggle with her over the price of eggs.

A similar truck would navigate through the narrow boreens of Ballylanders, the birthplace of my mother. This time it was Michael Walsh who would sell provisions to the farming families in this rural outpost.

Once again, my brother and I would circle the back of the truck where the sweets were kept as we waited for Granny Cleary to place her order.

"Aren't ye a little late today?" she might ask.

"Aye, I got caught up at the Sampsons," might come the exaggerated and exasperated reply. "Herself is sick to her stomach over the little wan coming home from the disco at all hours of the night. Ye've got to watch this younger crowd like a hawk."

"Yerra, the parish priest doesn't hear as many confessions as yerself," Granny might say, her lips pursing and her eyes rolling underneath the tight gray curls. "'If the stories had any weight to them, sure the tires would burst out from under you!"

Though Peapod allows the stay-at-home shopper an opportunity to click a mouse instead of clipping coupons and creeping through crowds, it will never have the neighborhood gossip morsels that are doled out at no charge from the back of an Irish traveling shop!

Irish Mammy Heroics

My colleague Paddy Clancy at IrishCentral.com reported recently that a study carried out at the Department of Psychology at the University of Limerick by lead researcher Elaine Kinsella said parents, particularly mothers, were regularly cited as heroes. Batman, Superman, and the entire Justice League were also mentioned on the list but were no match for the Irish mammy at the end of the day!

Kinsella said, "Traditional descriptions referred to heroes in masculine terms and often described those who risk their own lives to help others. But we found that although many types of heroes exist, the most frequently mentioned hero is one's mother."

When the research participants were asked to define heroic characteristics, they emphasized the need for evidence of self-sacrifice and moral integrity, qualities found in parents and mothers.

Had I been asked to partake in the survey, the definition of hero as described above would have probably led me to pick my Limerick-born mother as well. My mother has made sacrifices too numerous to mention in this limited space for the sake of her sons. Although we had an excellent school system in our town, my mother took extra shifts as a waitress to make sure there was enough to send us to the premier Catholic high school in the county. I've never met a more honest woman and to be sure, you have the best fighting chance in life when you have my mother in your corner. Maybe you don't always want to hear her advice (and quite often you get it even when you didn't ask for it), but her judgment is rock solid and the direction she gives is from a moral compass steeped in her deep Catholic faith. Even after she leaves this earth, it will be her voice inside my head that will keep me on the straight and narrow with a mixture of no-

nonsense common sense…and a pinch of Irish guilt for good measure!

Speaking of that little voice inside your head and the pinch of Irish guilt, I'm wondering if that was behind the overwhelming number of Irish sons who picked their mammy as their top hero over Batman. You can almost hear that voice go to work on the poor fella as he filled in the circles of the survey with his No. 2 pencil.

Batman is a fine choice for a hero, I suppose. He's a bit dark, though, isn't he? I remember ye being afraid of the dark and sure, I don't remember Batman or Robin signing up to strip the sheets after yeh wet yer bed when I shut out the lights.

The pencil would drift away from the Batman choice in favor of Superman instead. Not so fast!

Jaysis, I coulda used a Superman around the house when ye were growing up! He could have flown to the supermarket before it closed at 11 when you sprung on me at bedtime that you needed supplies for an art project that was due the next morning. He wasn't flyin' around the house when ye needed him most—that choice is almost as odd as yer man with the utility belt.

I suppose an Irish mammy might be able to live with Batman or Superman but God forbid you put another woman over her.

Wonder Woman?! Funny, I don't remember any girleen swooping in to rescue yeh with her invisible plane and lasso when Matthew McCabe was set to beat the stuffin' outta yeh when we lived on Liberty Avenue, but if that floozy really is your choice, fair play to yeh.

Batman had his gadgets, Wonder Woman had her lasso, and Superman had that strength and X-ray vision. But when the lead hit the paper on the survey, none of those superpowers is a match for an Irish mother's guilt!

A Lenten Pizza Penance

"I gave up social networking for Lent."

I posted this on my Facebook profile on the morning of Ash Wednesday and within seconds, got the following reply.

"Lent started already, dummy! You're not into it one day and already you have to find something new to give up."

It made me swallow hard on my Egg McMuffin, which I realized had meat in it. Right there, my brain on shamrocks kicks into guilt mode.

Perhaps your kind is more suited for Spy Wednesday, that little voice inside my head whispers in my ear. *That's the day before Holy Thursday, when Judas gave Jesus up. Enjoy that Canadian bacon now, luv, 'cos I don't think they serve that down below where yer goin'.*

When it comes to Lent, I just give up. Period.

It says on the AboutCatholics.com website: "Christian faithful are to do penance through prayer, fasting, abstinence and by exercising works of piety and charity during Lent. All Fridays through the year, and especially during Lent, are penitential days."

I can remember the penitential meals that were served on Fridays during Lent in my house. Though I grew up in a Jersey City neighborhood famous for having a killer pizzeria on virtually every corner, we did culinary penance with the English muffin pizza. The Irish mother's recipe went something like this in our house:

1. set oven to broil.

2. split all of the English muffins and place on a baking dish,

3. *uncap a large jar of Ragu marinara sauce, placing a dollop in the center of each muffin.*

4. *Release 8 slices of Kraft American cheese from the contents of their plastic sleeves.*

5. *Broil until cheese bubbles, about 10 minutes.*

Of course, the cheese was more processed than a Britney Spears vocal, which meant it only melted if it struck the surface of the sun. The poor English muffin would be charcoal bread long before the broiler got to work on the bright orange faux dairy blanket.

It wasn't until my cousin Rob married an Italian that we got a proper education on the sumptuous delights of snow-white shavings of mozzarella melting into the molten, slow-cooked Sunday gravy.

"Faith'n, ye all ate the Ragu that was put in front of yeh and it was good enough at the time," my Aunt Mary sniffed, finding the prospect of a daughter-in-law outgunning her in the kitchen too hard to swallow.

Can I count dodging my daughters' pointed questions about what I am giving up for Lent as penance enough? To them, Lent is an adventure in endurance—can a body really go without chocolate and iCarly reruns for 40 days?

Back in my day, we were all given small cardboard piggy banks and encouraged to beg on behalf of the "mission babies" in Africa during the Lenten season. I remember what a thrill it was when we hit $100 in donations as a class—that's when we got to name our very own mission babies! This was back in the 1970s, so I am sure there are plenty of middle-aged Africans running around the jungle angry at their parents for giving them names like Farrah, Fonz, Mork, Mindy, Laverne, and Shirley.

They would probably be a good deal angrier if they knew how many coins I siphoned off the top of the mission baby collection for ice cream and candy. Indeed, I have lots to atone for in my life. It makes a guy change his McDonald's order from a Big Mac to a Filet o' Fish on this particular Friday, just in case this whole Lenten sacrifice thing saves me from the fires of hell. I imagine having your soul broiled like an English muffin pizza would be just a tad painful....

Clouded Vision

My wife has left for the day to meet John Edward, the chipmunk-faced psychic and author of *Crossing Over*.

Hey, I'm psychic too and can tell what the future holds! I can predict that I will raise holy hell in the next two weeks when the credit card statement shows how much I got robbed for this bill of goods yer man is selling!

I am suspicious of John Edward. He targets women like my mother-in-law, who dragged my wife to this "private viewing" event at great expense in a frantic attempt to connect with her husband, the great man whom cancer ripped from our grasp so prematurely.

You could just picture this scene. "I'm not going to come to you through the mouth of that crook," my wife's formidable father, Richard, will yell out to his daughter and wife from a cloud during this psychic reading, ruffling a copy of today's *New York Times* as he crosses his long legs on the recliner.

I know Edward would never get a read on me because I am closed off to the possibility of such nonsense. But if I were open to it, I would direct his attention to a cloud next to Richard, where my grandmothers would meet for their daily tea. They got on well during their time on earth and I would hope this friendship would continue in these greener pastures.

"'Tis a nice girleen that Michael Joe married," my Granny Farragher would lean over and say to Granny Cleary about my wife as she scanned the event with her intense blue eyes. "Pity the cray-ture is gullible enough to fork over my grandson's money to this tinker."

"Yerra, Barbara is a dote," my Granny Cleary would chirp with a high voice. "Can yeh believe our Michael Joseph is coming out with a follow-up to the great smash *This Is Your Brain on Shamrocks*, and it'll be available on Kindles and online this February?"

Granny Cleary was always my biggest fan and would have definitely dropped that plug into a conversation! Besides, this is *my* psychic reading. Back off!

"There was always something about that boy alright, he never missed a trick when he came into my parlor," Granny Farragher might say, her wrinkled thumbs circling the rim on the mug of tea. "I should have known he'd be cataloging all of that detail for a book someday. Mind yeh, he could take off some weight, sure, he's big as a house."

"Och, sure, leave him be," Granny Cleary might say as she fussed with the kerchief atop her curly gray hair. "I think the weight suits him, like. Mind yeh, a little padding never hurt anyone."

"And how old were ye again when ye passed on from a heart attack, missus?"

"Sixty-five," would come the reply.

"Oh, right," Granny Farragher might say with a nod, the eyebrows dancing above her thick bifocals momentarily. She'd be discreet enough to bring the mug of tea up to her face to hide the protruding tongue in her cheek. "Yeh sure yeh have enough butter on that scone, pet?"

"I don't know why my Eileen worries about Michael Joseph so," Granny Cleary might say with an exasperated sigh and furrowed brow. "The lad and his brother turned out fine, sure! Stop mothering them already! Michael's got a great girl and they're doing a fine job raising the daughters, but still she has to nitpick about every little thing; Mass attendance, if they are wearing warm clothes, the pathway he shoveled in the snow is too narrow, and what the neighbors think about the gaudy inflatable Christmas decorations still buried on the front lawn under all that snow.

"Can yeh believe it? She runs around that house all day long worrying herself sick about these little things—imagines the state of her if her kids had real problems? Now she has *me* pacing the clouds about her! I hope she doesn't wind herself into an early grave with shot nerves!"

"'Tis a mystery where she got that trait from, missus," would come Granny Farragher's cool reply. "No idea a'tall, sure. Anyway, not a bother. Your Eileen will bury them all down there, fair play to her."

"I suppose," Granny Cleary would say. She would stand up, press the wrinkles out of her flowered dress with her hand, and walk over to the edge of the cloud.

"John Edward, if ye can hear me, have Barbara tell Eileen, Mick, and the kids we love them and can't wait to see them!"

"But not too soon, mind yeh, there'll be time enough for that," Granny Farragher might say from the table. "Let's say a prayer that they're all up here an hour before the divil knows they're dead. Now, come on, missus, the tea is getting cold. Don't pay no mind to that eejit down there."

Let's Toast the Pioneers!

Being a writer doesn't suck.

I'd be rich if I had a dime for every time a neighbor rings me up and asks for a meeting at the pub to punch up a resume or work on a proposal. On one such evening, my neighbor raised his glass in a toast.

"Two Irish guys that come from a long line of drunks—the tradition lives on!" He had a look of surprise and disappointment when I didn't lift my pint in response. I couldn't, you see, because that statement isn't true.

Both of my parents were Irish Pioneers that gave an oath to God around the time of their Confirmation to never touch a drop of alcohol. Many of my father's siblings and their children took the same oath.

According to the official Pioneer Association website, The Pioneer Total Abstinence Association of the Sacred Heart was founded in 1898 by the Wexford priest Fr. James Cullen S.J. in Dublin. As the story goes, his motivation in setting up the Pioneers was to address the enormous damage that he saw excess alcohol was doing in the Ireland of his times. Many workers were heavy drinkers, and alcohol was the greatest drain on the weekly earnings of the family. Members pledged three things: to abstain from alcohol for life (to which Fr. Cullen referred as "the heroic sacrifice"); to say the Pioneer prayer twice a day; and to bear witness by wearing the Pioneer pin at all times. The PTAA has always been underpinned by devotion to the Sacred Heart, and its emblem reflects this.

The existence of this organization comes as a complete surprise to the average Irish-American, and even to some Irish-born people I know. Yet a dry household is a critical element to my Irish upbringing and has produced some interesting Irish customs.

Until recently, my mother would write to the Hallmark Card Co. in protest over their portrayal of the Irish as drunks in their St. Patrick's Day greetings. Public displays of liver-abusing reindeer games never played well with my parents and we were always discouraged from public displays of consumption.

"Can yeh believe she's walkin' around like that?" my mother would huff, motioning her head in the direction of a bride gliding from table to table with a beer in her hand. "Shows no class a'tall. Some people think the only way to have a good time is to have a drink in their hand."

I don't remember being asked by either parent to join the Pioneer movement when I was being confirmed; I don't think I could have signed up for that. There are times when I wished I had because my liver is so big and black that it is aiming to qualify for the Jamaican bobsled team!

Coming to in a New Orleans gutter as a drug-addicted drag queen rifles through your pants pocket for a wallet and God knows what else is one time when being a Pioneer would have been a good thing.

Waking up next to what looked like a warthog with lace undergarments caught in her tusks is another time that being a Pioneer would have been a good thing.

Steadying yourself with one hand on the steering wheel and one hand on a bottle of Windex as you gamely attempt to wipe the dried vomit from the carpet of your wife's brand new car while your head throbs mercilessly is yet another instance where being a Pioneer would have been a good thing.

You get the idea.

If I know my mother, she just read the last few paragraphs and said aloud to no one, "the eejit didn't get that example from his parents!" As usual, my mother is right on the money.

"Lead me not into temptation, I can find it myself," is a twist on the Lord's Prayer that I usually utter before a shot of Jameson's goes down the gullet, and truer words have never been spoken. Despite the pristine example of clean living set by my parents, the bottle has tempted me into dark neighborhoods and it hasn't always been easy to throw the car into reverse gear. I never had to visit church basements except for fundraising suppers, and for that I thank the Lord. Speaking of the man upstairs, I've asked the Lord to take the wheel in those dark neighborhoods and you reading this is proof that Jesus has mad stunt-driving skills.

I was a bartender once, which is never a good profession when the bottle calls as loudly as it sometimes does. Back then, club soda was my best friend because it looked like a real drink when you dropped a wedge of lime into it.

"Let's rework that toast," I say as the bartender responds to my call for a club soda in a pint glass. "To the Pioneers and their sacrifices— let's pray they gain entry into heaven a full half-hour before the devil knows they're dead!"

Now *that* is something I'll drink to!

What Will the Neighbors Think?

Anyone with Irish blood in their veins has heard those five words strung in an accusatory question from their parents at one time or another.

You come home with long hair and a piercing from college. You get off the tarmac at the Aer Lingus terminal packing a chin that wasn't there the last time you were in Ireland. You're in counseling and popping antidepressants like Pez. News of a rough spot in your marriage gets out. Or, the Lord save us and guard us, you write about any of the above "family business" topics in a book like this. No matter the circumstance, a furrowed brow and a shot of worry about what others will think about this latest development is the Irish knee-jerk reaction to every twist and turn of life's road.

Of course, each one of those "neighbors" in the parish of my youth have skeletons in their closet that could outpace the jigs and reels that our family's skeletons have done in the dark corners of our house. But that didn't seem to matter as we, growing up, sterilized the rough spots in our lives and appearance before leaving the house so that the best possible image was put forth into the world.

Y'know, I thought I mothballed my rebellious streak when I graduated college twenty-some years ago. It began raging in the last few weeks as the *This Is Your Brain on Shamrocks* book tour kicked off at the same time that a select few in my family sat on the sidelines worrying what the neighbors would think of the perceived vulgarities in the book. In a weird way, it fueled a fire in me to get that thing in as many hands as possible, so I thank the (precious few) naysayers in my clan for the misplaced but much-needed inspiration behind all the perspiration.

The month of September 2001 has dark significance in the world, but it has an element of joy and rebirth for me. That was the month that two significant conversations enabled me to break free from a life that had manufactured a charade to please a collection of people about whose opinion I could not care less.

I had gone to a coaching course called The Landmark Forum the weekend before the towers fell and the instructor encouraged us to reflect on how much time we had spent trying to look good and avoid looking bad. When you're Irish and forced to spend a weekend taking inventory of what you invested in that ridiculous and vicious cycle, you are struck with how many years you robbed yourself of power, freedom, and self-expression in your life. It boggles the mind and I resolved never to put those confines on myself again.

Of course, the tragic events of 9/11 taught us that life was too short. How many people wondered about what the neighbors thought of their life as they met such a grisly death in the Pentagon that day? I rest my case.

I guess I was still in that self-awareness fog a few days later when I met Sir Bob Geldof for coffee in midtown Manhattan. I remember marveling how his disheveled hair matched the grey pinstripes of his Savile Row jacket perfectly. I was interviewing him for this column about *Sex, Age & Death*, a highly personal album he had just released and which addressed the suicide of his ex-wife and the affair she had with INXS frontman Michael Hutchence. During our chat I had the temerity to ask him what he thought the family would think of the lyrics.

"I could give two shites about that," he said with a sneer. "You worry about what the neighbors think and art dies. *You* die. I never would have accomplished Live Aid or anything else in my life if I thought much about looking bad or feeling a failure."

Let that sink in for a moment. Thousands of Africans were saved because one Irishman pushed through the worry about how he would be perceived. I was so inspired that I gave birth to my writer self there, in that afternoon. It was no longer enough to be a scribbler who merely comments on the creations of others as a music critic. It had suddenly become critical that I transform into someone who creates something unique.

I rolled up my sleeves that day and published my first novel, *Collared*, within 18 months of meeting Geldof and doing my work in the Landmark classes. This new pathway of unconstrained self-expression through writing has added dimensions of joy and creativity to my life that I cannot possibly describe in this space.

You're holding in your hand the sequel to the collection of essays from my second book, *This Is Your Brain on Shamrocks*. Readers see the love and wit of their deceased mother in how I describe my living mom in these essays, and they tell me it moved them to tears. They hear an essay about my deceased Uncle Bob in Yonkers and Bob is brought to life once again on McLean Avenue as someone recalls hearing his band The Limerick Weavers. Above all, they reflect on the common themes of family, guilt, love, and unity that run through our lives.

The subsequent book tour taught me that being a writer means a dedication to writing things that *make* your neighbors think, without worrying much about what they'll think about you. I wouldn't live my life any other way.

Remembering "The Cross Woman"

My Aunt Mary got her name "the cross woman" from my cousin Noreen's small tykes. To her, Mary was the old aunt from America who wouldn't tolerate little boys horsing around the house. One look and a curt "knock it off" spit through gritted teeth put them in their place.

I knew that look well. She could pierce with that emerald-eye gaze when we acted up as kids. She would cock an eyebrow and glare at you like a falcon inspecting a baby rabbit with a broken foot. It was a look that displayed both her impatience and disbelief that such an unwashed heathen had dropped from her family tree.

I am envious of her. As a parent, I have tried unsuccessfully to perfect that withering glance, and my kids ride all over me no matter how coldly I gaze in their direction.

We were gathered as a family on a recent Sunday at the 9 AM Mass in her parish to honor Mary on the fifth anniversary of her passing. You could almost feel her in the pew with us, the no-nonsense Irish matriarch whose direct, fair, and loving influence was so strong that she kept all of us on the straight and narrow half a decade following her sudden death.

Her best friend, Bernadette, came to the house for tea after Mass. I introduced myself to her as Mary's nephew, to which she replied, "Why wouldn't I know you? Sure, I read ye every week in the *Irish Voice* and mind yeh, there are some weeks that I don't care for yeh at all."

No wonder Mary got along so well with this woman. Like Bernadette, Mary called it as she saw it without thinking of how it might land over there because the filter between her brain and mouth was either nonexistent or hopelessly clogged. Children of Irish mothers know well what I mean here.

I was a bit nervous about putting Mary in the same room as my wife's grandmother on our wedding day. Baba, as she was called, loved to tell the tale of red-headed boys throwing rocks at the only Jewish girl in Kansas. "Two things I can't stand are prejudiced people and the Irish," she would say. You could imagine how my courtship went.

I winced as Mary and Baba chatted at the perimeter of the dance floor because I was a nervous wreck overall at my wedding at the prospect of this uneasy Catholic/Jewish family connection. I was terrified by the notion of those two queens crossing swords.

Mary soon returned to "our side" of the room, sat in her chair, and tucked her slip under her red dress before nodding in Baba's direction.

"That's a woman who speaks her mind," she declared. "Sure, there's not enough of us in the world anymore." With that, the ice melted between the Irish and Jews as we found a common ground in our servitude to straight-talking elder stateswomen. In subsequent family gatherings, the two were inseparable.

Mary was actually quite kind and selfless, a model servant of the Lord whose faith sustained her in the best and worst of times. She was not cross, but you could see how a kid could think that way about her. Mary was just an extremely practical woman who thought it was ridiculous to cater on every whim of a child who should be seen and not heard.

There are hilarious home videos of my cousin Robert unwrapping the same fire truck under the Christmas tree year after year; he was so overwhelmed with the bounty that he never missed it. "Sure, how much can a kid really play with before they become overloaded?" she said with a huff once in her defense while we joked around her about the shameless "re-gifting."

I can remember vividly a time when she threw Rob's hockey equipment out of his third-floor bedroom and onto the concrete patio below in another lesson of no-bull parenting.

"What are you doing?" Rob screamed. "You could have broken these things! They are worth hundreds of dollars!"

"Are they?" she shouted, hurling the hockey sticks out the window as she spoke. "How was I to know that? They were just lying around the floor after I told you five times to pick them up and care for them. You treated this stuff like junk, so I assumed it was."

I can't remember ever seeing the hockey gear lying around ever again, proving that this cross woman was someone you'd never want to cross.

The Tough Man with the Soft Center

We all have those moments when our life flashes before our eyes as we face a certain death—a car crash, scaffolding drops in front of you on the sidewalk—you get the idea.

The first time I can remember that moment of pure terror was in the half bathroom of my Uncle John's basement. I was playing hide-and-seek with my cousins and in my rush to find a hiding place, I pushed the door and put the knob through the wall.

I had visions of a scourge and public crucifixion on Uncle John's front lawn for the crime of ruining his immaculately painted drywall, and I avoided that fate by moving one of the hand towels on the towel bar so that it covered up the hole, leaving the door open, and hiding someplace else. When I went to their house the next time, the hole was filled in with perfectly sanded spackle and painted over with the exact shade of white, as if nothing had happened.

I was terrified of what John would do because he was the intense brother of my father of whom every kid in the family was petrified. He resembled the Jack Russell terriers he kept as pets in his later years: compact and high-strung, an animal you couldn't pet without the threat of having an Achilles tendon ripped from your leg if you made the wrong move. He had the same owlish, wide blue eyes as his mother, and they sat underneath a widow's peak of hair held in place with Brylcreem at all times.

Come to think of it, everything was held in place when it came to John. The house was impeccable at all times, despite three kids under 10 running around. The lawn was a carpet without a blade bent the wrong way and the garden would make any thumb green with envy.

There was also a master plan to his life that he executed flawlessly. He came to America at 20, worked at a relentless pace on the New Jersey Turnpike for twenty years, and saved enough money to build a stunning home in the hills of his beloved County Galway where he lived out his last years.

There wasn't an hour of overtime that would go unworked on the Turnpike if John knew about it. My dad likes to tell the story of John working double time and a half on Christmas Eve at the Jersey City interchange and a fellow toll collector asking him why he wasn't home with his kids on the holidays. "Yerra, we don't go for that stuff where we come from in Ireland," he said, winking at my dad at the next toll booth. "What I did was I took the kids to Two Guys earlier today and had them run around with the toys in the aisles and sure, isn't that good enough for them?"

He was so intense that when he made a joke like this, you wouldn't know if he was pulling your leg and that made the punch line even funnier. One time, I stood with him and my wife near a stone wall as we waved at my cousin's bridal motorcade. My wife plucked a few blackberries from the vines woven through the cobblestones and remarked to John how good they were. "Aye," he said with a straight face. "'Tis the cows pissing on them that give them that tart taste, like." My wife abruptly spat them out as the rest of us roared.

True to the master plan, he moved back home to Ireland at the age of forty and it was there that I met the other side of my uncle. He would dismiss you with an "ah, g'wan" when you dared suggest you would rent a car from Dan Dooley's Rental, insisting instead on picking you up at Shannon Airport. "Welcome home," he'd whisper in your ear with a broad smile as you met his firm handshake with a hug. And Uncle John would melt in an inconsolable puddle of tears when it was time to take you back to the airport a week later, revealing himself to be the kindest and most sensitive soul of the Farragher clan underneath that flimsily gruff exterior.

His master plan went off the rails one morning, just days after his 60th birthday, when the Lord took him home before his lifeless body could hit the floor of his daughter's barn.

I feel that loss the most when I land in Shannon, crane my neck for any signs of him, and see his wife or adult children instead. Everything is in place at the gravesite, with an impeccably kept plot and a lacquered black-marble headstone with an embedded picture of John smiling at you. Now, it's me who sheds the tears when I leave his plot.

Though he has been dead for over a decade, there is still a hole in our hearts that no amount of time or spackle could ever fill.

The Cross with a Prize Inside

Through a confluence of events not worth getting into right now, I find myself sleeping in my parents' bed tonight. As I peel back the covers I look up above the headboard and catch a glimpse of the Last Rights Crucifix.

It's beautiful: vintage heavy walnut with a brass Jesus hanging in agony, as is the custom. Like a box of Cracker Jacks, our Savior is hiding a prize inside! But this is a prize you don't want to open anytime soon.

When you grab the base of His feet and slide Him up the cross, a small compartment reveals itself with a pair of candles, a small vial of holy water, and a yellowed instruction sheet that guides the reader through the sacrament of Last Rites.

Ghastly is the word that comes to mind as I inspect this—it's like the Grim Reaper's utility belt. I can't imagine a circumstance where I'd get to use this. God forbid I wake up one day and my wife is cold to the touch beside me. I'm sure I'll be wrestling with shock and nausea over having slept with a dead body all night. Necrophilia ain't my bag and I'm certain I'll be busy in the shower with the steam on trying to get the dead cooties off me while I await an ambulance. I'm not going anywhere near my wife's cold, dead forehead to make the Sign of the Cross with holy water and it is now that I thank the Lord once again that she is Jewish and doesn't believe in the cross to begin with.

For the benefit of my wife or anyone else who wanders into my bedroom and finds me unconscious, it is my final wish that you call 911 immediately and use those paddles to shock my fat pasty white ass back to life. Of course, modesty prevents me from sleeping in the nude, so you won't have to worry about covering me up in any way. Now is not the time to be running around the house looking for a Bic and fumbling with the candles to perform a ceremony best done by a priest!!

Besides, I am so riddled with sin that St. Peter's gonna have plenty of material to go through before making a final judgment on where I will spend eternity.

Origins:

DC Comics rebooted your favorite superheroes last year with "the New 52" series, giving fresh coats of paint and new story lines to the likes of Superman and Wonder Woman. It reminded me how much I loved reading about the origins of those characters as a kid and how fascinated I was with the pain that drove the likes of billionaire Bruce Wayne to strike fear in criminals' hearts by dressing like a giant bat.

There were some recent events that made me reflect on my own origins. The first was a series of interviews that the New York University Glucksman Ireland House conducted with my parents and myself as part of their Oral History Collection.

The Ireland House is doing the Lord's work preserving the histories of authors, clergy, bricklayers, and everyone in between with this series. Hearing my parents' stories told in their own words was an indescribable thrill and provides my family with an oral history of our own that will be passed down to subsequent generations.

I heard the origin of my family in their recount. The sadness of watching the farm in the rearview mirror as my grandparents drove them to Shannon Airport soon faded in the face of a new world's bright promise and modern accoutrements. In this sharing, I can see origins of my own sense of adventure. I heard the origins of my sly sense of humor in my father's response to the question as to the credit he gives his friend for introducing him to my mother at a wedding. "Yerra, there are days I blame him as well," he says. The good-natured laughter between dad and his missus that immediately followed that joke provides an origin to the easy relations between my wife and me.

I hear the origins of the keen writer's eye for observation and detail in listening to mom's gentle whispers in my father's ear throughout the interview as she corrects his occasional lapses in facts.

The interviewer peppers me with questions during our session, and it brings back memories and introduces new observations long buried or never realized. I'm reminded of the envelopes of waitressing tips my mother put under the blotter of the dining room table; one was labeled "trip to Ireland" and another one might say "poles" as she funded a telephone line off the main road and through the narrow boreen to her mother's house. In that memory I also see the origins of my own obsession with saving for retirement and keeping debt levels low in a house full of ravenous teenage consumerism.

With my last trip to Ireland for the book tour, I can see the origins of what made me the person I am today with my own two eyes. It hit me during a bittersweet visit that had me stare into the faraway gaze of my maternal grandmother's sister, Peggy. We both giggle spontaneously as she walks through the door of the pub and I smile broadly at our mutual tendency of approaching each social situation with the enthusiasm of a tickled toddler. Her mind has faded after almost nine decades, yet I can still see the origins of my own mischievous spark in the eye as she is about to assemble a good yarn while stirring her tea.

The origins of my sharp tongue and quick wit come into focus when my dad's family gathers at my book signing in Tuam. When David Burke, the editor of *The Tuam Herald*, turns and asks my 81-year-old bachelor uncle where his wife was, he shakes his head. "Well, the girleen hasn't been born yet and her mother's dead," came the instant reply.

I lean over the headstone of my paternal grandmother's grave and I can't tell if the wind rustles the dry leaves or if that was her voice whispering. "Nice piece in the *Herald* about the book—aren't ye the humble one? And peddling the book in the church parking lot after

Mass was a grand gesture altogether." I make the Sign of the Cross and laugh to myself. No mystery where my tendency to get the last word comes from! Having your say when you're six feet under is indeed a miracle, yet I expect nothing less from Brigid Farragher.

I am grateful that my family origins contain so many amazing people who never wore a mask or cape but are superheroes nonetheless.

A Name By Any Other Name!

One of my most memorable Thanksgiving weekends was the one I spent with cousins I never knew I had! I met a lovely man from my old Hudson County stomping grounds at one of my book signings over the summer, who proceeded to blog about the book and our meeting on the Jersey City Facebook page that he runs. A woman I did not know replied to his post, "OMG! I think this is my cousin!"

A cousin I didn't know about in Jersey City? Impossible!

"Yeah, we have some McNaught cousins," my dad confirmed flatly when I mentioned Donna's name, not offering much detail as to why we never connected. "Your aunt had more to do with them than I did."

We discovered that we both lived in Monmouth County and lunch at a nearby Perkins was arranged a week later. Donna walked in and I could see no family resemblance whatsoever. She had an olive complexion kissed by the sun that was in stark contrast to my pink and freckled skin. As we began our excited and rapid-fire exchange, however, it was clear there was a lot of common ground. We went to the same grammar school, had the same teachers, were pathologically cheery and outgoing, and came from good, hardworking stock that ensured Irish roots were planted deep inside their children.

"I have a question I've been dying to ask," Donna said before the waitress could even take our order. "Why is your last name Farragher and my mother's maiden name Farrington?"

My father's uncle—Donna's grandfather—Darby had come across the Atlantic in the 1930s and had changed his name to Farrington in an attempt to blend in. With St. Patrick's Day parades down Fifth Avenue and Irish pride stronger than ever, it seems inconceivable in this day and age to conceal your Irish heritage in the American melting pot, but prejudice against the Irish was strong back then and that's what had to be done to survive in the new land. My dad's older sister Mary came to America in the early 1950s at a time when the effects of the "no Irish need apply" ethos were a not-too-distant memory and she listed Farrington as her last name as well. By the time my dad entered the United States later that decade, jobs were plentiful for the Irish and he had more of a say in the matter of keeping the family birth name.

We decided to reunite our parents at our next meeting and Donna's mother, Audrey, came to my house for a barbecue. There was a tough Irish-American matriarch under that thatch of supernaturally dyed red hair and she was not buying into this explanation of why our names were different. "Your family changed *your* name before you came over," she said, wagging a finger toward us. She was becoming visibly upset at my father's explanation.

"You remember Peggy Ford?" my dad asked.

"Of course," Audrey huffed.

"Her family's name was Rabbitte and they changed it when they came over," my dad explained. "The only Ford ye'll find in Ireland is parked in a garage!"

Audrey took this as more blasphemy and my father, allergic as he is to conflict, smiled politely and kept his tongue until they left—but just barely.

Of course, the practice of changing names predates my Grand-Uncle Darby. Author Darren McGettigan blogs on the FamilyHistoryIreland.com site that the first signs of change in Irish surnames actually began with the mass dropping of the O and Mc prefixes to many names during Elizabethan times. The Tyrone surnames McGawell and O'Gormley became Campell and Grimes, for example.

It was interesting to hear the plausible family legends that sprang from this name change when the larger group of cousins met over the weekend.

"He changed his name even before he hit Ellis Island is what I heard," said one cousin. "No, Darby was running from the Black and Tans and made his way over to Scotland, probably because he was running away from something or someone," reasoned another in a more dashing interpretation of family history.

Although the reasons why names were changed and the opinions on who has the "correct" last name may never be resolved between my dad and his cousin, it allows their offspring a space to share in a wicked humor that is a universal family trait.

"We'll have to do this again soon, only bigger," my cousin Donna said as she kissed me good-bye. "And next time, we'll make the reservation under Farrington!" A name is but a name. I'm counting the days!

Judging the Wake

Note: I heard some amazing stories at a recent family gathering about Irish mothers and their wakes. Allow me to paint the picture as it was painted to me by an able storyteller whose name is being protected out of fear that his dead mother will come back to haunt him.

The air was heavy with sugary pollen that clung to the heavy red velvet drapes. The body would be couched inside the pillowy lining of the lacquered coffin, open, of course. Rows of cheap wooden chairs were set up in front of it. The Irish widow patted the hand of the funeral director, barely mustering the strength to mouth the words "thank you" in her deep grief.

Someone had dropped a pill in her sweaty palm a while back "to calm the auld nerves," and things were moving in slow motion for the old gal. She nodded approvingly at her son as he walked toward her in a pressed black suit with matching tie. They were alone and she said a private prayer of thanks that the shrew of a daughter-in-law would be too busy with little kids at home to show her ungrateful face. He dutifully hooked his arm at his side and his mother slid her gloved hand inside it as they made their way toward the coffin. He was guiding her to the kneeler by his father but felt a pull toward the flowers. She removed her reading glasses from her small purse, balanced them on her nose, squinted, and fingered the cards tucked inside the bouquets.

"Ah, jaysis, would you look at this feckin' nonsense," she said with a heavy sigh. "All this money for something that will be dead in two days, the Lord save us and guard us. Such a waste."

She shook her head.

"Well, if ye were gonna spend this amount anyways, ye'd think yer wan would have gotten a better bouquet! Sure, didn't yer father get him his first job when he came over from Connemara at the American Can Company? And this is the feckin' thanks he gets?"

"Ma, please," the son pleaded in hushed whispers. "It's the thought that counts."

"Exactly!" came the hissed reply as she fingered the hem of the altar vestments that hung on a wire dummy in the middle of the flowers. "Now this is how ye do it. Yeh paying attention? Yeh can never go wrong with vestments. Spend the extra money on vestments and avoid this flower nonsense."

She snatched another card from the bouquet and grimaced.

"Some people have gumption, I tell yeh," she said through clenched teeth. "His sister sends the biggest bouquet in the place to draw attention to herself. Flowers instead of making the trip over. And who would want to see that old crow anyway, squawking about the family business to anyone that'd listen to her like a wet magpie on a telephone wire."

She bent her head and fumbled in her purse momentarily before pressing a wrinkled piece of paper into her son's hand.

"Listen, I need you to do something."

"Anything, Ma."

"Ye'll need to keep the seating arrangements straight. Mary's family is in the row behind me at the wake and the cemetery. Bridie's clan is behind that. I could care less who sits behind that but if we don't get those two rows straight, I'll never hear the end of it."

"Ma, that's ridiculous!"

"Yerra, it is not," she said defiantly. "Please just do this to keep the peace around here—yer father would have wanted it this way and sure I don't want to add to his worries in that coffin."

You cannot make this stuff up.

When I Was Your Age....

There's a great date-night venue that my wife and I frequent, called the Silver Ball Museum in Asbury Park, New Jersey. $10 buys you a half hour of unlimited games on vintage pinball and video-game machines.

I found myself standing in front of the Gorgar pinball game, and it was a trip down memory lane. Gorgar was a red muscular demon with scantily clad women worshiping at his feet in the artwork on the machine. It was built in 1979, the year I was 13. It was a big deal when the first one was shipped to my mall, because it was one of the first talking pinball machines. Because microchips were so primitive at the time, Gorgar only said a few unintelligible words.

Before the half hour ended, I challenged my wife to a game of Asteroids. Some of you may recall this early video game—a rudimentary triangle of a spaceship that flies around a black and white screen, and you must break up the rocks in space using round bullets that shoot out of the top of the triangle before the rocks break you!

We got home and found our kids down in the basement, as usual, playing "Dance Dance Revolution" on their Wii console. The dancers are in vivid color and their moves are perfectly synched to those of my daughters, thanks to this nifty wireless wand technology in their hands.

You know what comes next.

"Wow," says I. "You know, when I was your age, we played video games on a black-and-white television—heck, we had to practically have our noses to the screen because the joystick was connected to the console with this short little wire. We didn't have wireless wands in our day!"

Yup. You guessed it. I became my father at that moment. Except I sounded like a whiny little d-bag delivering my video game tale of woe compared to the stories of his rough childhood in rural Galway during the 1940s.

I would remember my father shaking his head at the doorway in disgust while my brother and I played Atari video games after school back in the 1970s. "When I came home from school there were no video games," he said. "We would go straight to the bog and cut turf." My eye-roll took my focus off the screen and I'd lose the round, as he went on and on about it.

Dad would tell us how they hand-dug the first 12 inches to clean the bog before throwing it into the bog hole. They would then cut the turf, throwing it up on the bank sod by sod, and then pitchfork it and wheel it out to the plains for drying. Cutting and footing the turf and then loading it onto the cart where the horse or ass would pull it was even more backbreaking then the pitchforking process.

"We weren't up half the night talking to our friends on the phone," he'd say. "By jaysis, your head hit the pillow nice and early after that kind of afternoon. Even before I was old enough to cut turf, I had to go to the well to get the water to make the tea and then walk a mile to take the tea and the mugs and the bread and the jam over to my father and the workers." *Yeah, yeah. Whatever, Dad. You just screwed up my high score on Pong! Thanks a lot!*

On the rare occasions when the turf story got old or my father got tired, my mother might enter the ring with stories about her Octobers spent digging potatoes after school in Ballylanders, a hayseed outpost near Limerick. The good news about picking potatoes is that you may have gotten some time off from school. The bad news was that you would spend hours at a time digging in the dirt and kneeling on canvas sacks to keep the moisture from your knees after the threshing mill—a luxury—had its way with the rich soil. Try straightening your back after spending the afternoon hunched over the dirt amidst damp, chilly County Limerick air.

Most parents of a certain age love to spin that yarn of walking to school "uphill, both ways," as the comedian Bill Cosby once said. My parents are no exception. When I moan to them about taking out a home equity line of credit to fund the insatiable American Eagle appetite of two teenage girls, I am rewarded with a story of how lucky my parents were to have a pair of cheap green plastic Wellington boots that kept the dampness at bay during those mile-long walks to school in the rain.

Many of the same stories were corroborated by a book written by the Abbeyknockmoy Social Club for Retired People called *Shared Memories: Memories of Life in Rural Ireland.* To prove their point, even the book itself is primitive, printed in black and white and bound with staples to produce something you could make at a copy shop. I'm taking a Jimmy Dean lowfat ham and egg breakfast sandwich out of the microwave as I flip through the section in this book about killing the pig. It says here that the best female "crayture" weighing 18 stone would be fed oatmeal for a month, singled out, tied with a rope at the mouth, pierced in the main artery of the neck as blood drained into buckets, all before boiling water was poured over the pig to make the shaving process easier. After reading about how the pig's stomach would be cut to get the intestines for the black pudding, I'll be thinking twice before buying a frozen brick of that stuff for my St. Patrick's Day breakfast!

The stories about farm work, traveling carts, and calving were all pointless yarns that annoyed me to no end and got in the way of my video-game addiction. I wouldn't give a Canadian quarter—the pinball machine only took American quarters, you see—for this nonsense as a teenager. Now, as my parents and I face the reality of having many more yesterdays than tomorrows, those slices of oral history about the past become as precious as gold bricks. Though my stories of hardship pale in comparison to those of Mom and Dad, I suppose I try to impart a sense of historical perspective to my kids to confirm just how good they've got it in the same way that my parents did for me.

As they said in the old days, "Black cats have black kittens!"

Book 2: Remarks on an Unremarkable Life

I've heard it said that writers exist to help us make sense of our lives, providing a mirror image of ourselves and the times we live in.

As for myself, I think I get paid to sift through the monotonous minutiae of our everyday routines and then make something meaningful or funny out of it. Here are some attempts at that.

Have Mercy in the Parking Lot!

In an attempt to burn off some calories in combat with some especially gluttonous vacation consumption, I found myself this morning biking through the seaside mansions of Avalon. This ritzy enclave is a favorite vacation spot of the well-to-do from Philadelphia; I got in on the action because I am not ashamed of sponging off my wealthier in-laws.

As I pedaled off the pounds, I saw flashing lights ahead. There was a significant police presence blocking off the road. Was a preppy riot about to breakout over a heated game of cricket?
Close, but no. It was just the 10:30 AM Mass letting out.

Every member of my parish backs their car into the parking space as opposed to pulling the car in the spot headlong; good luck trying to find another parishioner willing to wait while you make a reverse K-turn out of your spot once the priest advises us to go in peace to love and serve the Lord!

The people in the pew next to you may dig deep into their pockets after some missionary lays it on thick with a sob story about starving African babies swatting away the flies as they eat their gruel, but there is no Catholic compassion in the parking lot once Mass lets out!

It reminds me of Father Hirsch, our cranky pastor in the parish of my teenage years. He would refuse to allow his flock to shake hands during the Sign of Peace during the Mass. "How hypocritical is that when you're going to try to kill one another to get out of the parking lot in the next fifteen minutes?" We all thought he was heartless at the time, but I think he might have a point as I survey the parade of cars honking as one driver takes his sweet time trying to make a left out of the church lot on this summer morning.

While there is no mention of road rage in the Bible, there are some lessons one can apply to steering-wheel etiquette.

Romans 12:10 says, "Love one another with brotherly affection. Outdo one another in showing honor."

Tell that to the guy who just flipped me the bird when I chanced pedaling too close to his gold-trimmed Cadillac!

Farewell to a Fashionista

You remember how that joke about *Playboy* magazine goes, when a husband claims to "look at it just for the articles" when his wife catches him with the goods? I feel like that when I have to defend why titles like *GQ, Esquire,* and *Details* are draped over the magazine rack in our downstairs bathroom.

Truth is, I really do read them for the articles now; there is some mighty fine writing therein about some of the weird things going on in America. Cults, serial killers, mob survival tactics, corporate espionage, and political corruption are just some examples of the news you can use, with stories not covered anywhere else.

Sure, there was a time when I used to subscribe to these rags as my *couture* compass, but I am long past that stage of my life.

I can remember the time and place when I decided I was no longer hip and fashionable. Glenn "The Style Guy" O'Brien, one of my favorite columnists for *GQ,* had just put an end to what I was convinced was the greatest men's fashion trend of this new century: the un-tucked shirt. His answer, *"The rule is: Tuck in your goddamn shirt, barn boy! But seriously, folks, I know that the hip thing has been to go around with your shirt out, or maybe half tucked, like you slept in your clothes and haven't had coffee yet. But this 'hip' look has been hip so long, how much longer can it possibly be hip?"*

I was crushed. It was all well and good when O'Brien would rip into some rube for wearing a mullet with overalls, but now the dude was hitting me where I live! This was my look! Letting the shirt hang out allowed me to let it all hang out way past the rim of my expandable waist pants. Now, I'd have to tuck it all in and let the shirt buttons creak under the weight!

From that point forward, I remember eyeing the suit models on the glossy pages with contempt. With their high cheekbones, coltish necks, and pale complexions, they looked more like concentration camp victims than runway thoroughbreds. Women of a certain roundness were celebrated in the paintings of Sir Peter Paul Rubens and that brought on what we now know to be the Rubenesque period of the 1600s; hundreds of years later, we're still waiting for men's magazines to celebrate the likes of Kevin James, Kevin Smith, and John Goodman as sex gods!

Of course, most manufacturers are missing a huge market. I love Calvin Klein clothes but most of them have a "slim fit cut." Really? With two-thirds of the world classified as overweight by the National Institutes of Health, you've just sewn up a very small market with this line of clothes!

It's not just the weight that keeps me from chasing the latest trends; age also has something to do with it. I just can't wear sandals known as 'mandals' with the painful heel spurs of my plantar fasciitis. I would look like a complete douche in the salmon-striped seersucker shorts I saw the young-uns wear at a recent high school graduation party. Rugby shirts make me look like the guy who stopped chasing the ball years ago. I have found refuge in surf shops, where drawstrings and flowy shirt designs are a guy's best friend. Even there, I have to stay clear of certain trends, like tank tops. With my pale and non-defined arms, sprigs of back hair, and skin tags under my arms that look like I'm smuggling a quart of strawberries, I have let go of the notion of ever wearing them.

I was reminded at the airport recently that I have an accessory that never goes out of style. I was trying to get onto an earlier flight when the woman at the US Airways counter asked me if I was a gold or silver flier. "No, I replied, but I have heard it is damn near impossible to refuse a man with dimples."

"They always make the man, sugar, come this way," was her reply. I chose the latest issue of *GQ* from the stack of available magazines as I settled into my seat in flrst class, feeling sorry for the poor sullen-looking waifs who got herded into coach class that day. You're never fully dressed without a smile!

Late Ain't Great

Here's one definition of insanity: going back to school in your middle age for a master's degree.

Here's a definition of stupidity: seating your fat married arse in a restaurant with a woman half your age to whom you are *not* married, and have her blurt out, "Omigod, I think I'm pregnant" loud enough to make every diner in the place turn around.

I had met Tina (not her real name) over dinner to study for a class we were both taking and I had noticed that she couldn't concentrate on anything. When I asked her to focus, she burst into tears.

"I had sex—and lots of it—over the holidays," she said between heaving sobs. "I wasn't careful. Now I'm late!"

Ah, youth. Here I thought I had a pretty nifty Christmas when Santa brought a big-screen TV down the chimney! I wondered briefly about exchanging my gift for the kind of Christmas she got, but thought better of it. But I digress.

"There's a Walgreen's next door," said I. "Go in there and buy a pregnancy test. If it's negative, we can get back to work and later you can reflect on how lucky you are to have dodged a bullet. If you're pregnant, then let's stop our study party here and you take care of whatever you need to take care of."

She went inside and I went to my car to wait for her. As I drummed my thumbs on the steering wheel, I looked around the parking lot. The hair rose on the back of my neck and I was convinced that Chris Hansen from *Dateline* would pop out from behind a parked car or Joey Greco's mobile-detective van from *Cheaters* would screech next to my driver's side door.

"Subject was seen at 7:30 PM at a Muscle Maker's Grill with a woman half his age," the voiceover would say as the camera rolled and the crew rushed my car. "A heated conversation about their relationship ensued and the tear-stained alleged mistress stumbled into a drugstore for a pregnancy test."

Thank God my wife is an understanding woman, and thank God for the girl's sake that my mother didn't come to our study party.

"Well, 'tis good you keep the hair so long, luv," Mom might have said to her. "That length sure came in handy when the sinner Mary Magdalene wiped Jesus' feet with it to atone for her sins."

Is there anything like an Irish matriarch to extinguish all urges with a little biblical reference? My mother would pace the margins of the dance floor as I "wang-chunged tonight" with my date during the Immaculate Conception school dances in the early 1980s.

"There is room for the Holy Spirit between the two of yeh, right?" she would coo in my ear as I got a bit too close to my date for her liking during a slow jam.

I swore I wouldn't go that route when it was my time to police a teen. I saw the young lady emerge from the bathroom with a relieved look, so I figured I'd try on my modern parent's speech in preparation for my soon-to-be sexually active teens.

"If you were trying to get pregnant, then what you did was responsible behavior," I said. "Was it your intention to get pregnant?"

"Of course not," she replied, rolling her eyes. "I was drunk and it just happened." I put up my hand in protest.

"Then what we have here is irresponsible behavior, plain and simple. You're a great girl with a great future and you are so responsible with studying that this way of being doesn't match who I know you to be."

In a move that might prove to the other diners beyond any reasonable doubt that we were having an affair, she leaned over and gave me a peck on my cheek.

"Thanks for setting me straight without judging me," she said.

It's like my homeboy St. Matthew said in 12:36-37. "I tell you, on the day of judgment, people will give account for every careless word they speak, for by your words you will be justified, and by your words you will be condemned."

With that, I got an amen and the check!

Tom Jones and the "Commando" Performance

To assuage the ingrained Irish Catholic guilt I sometimes feel when I miss Mass on Sunday, I put on spiritual music. A dash of Ronan Tynan's read of "Ave Maria," a pinch of Susan Boyle singing "How Great Thou Art," a few mumbled Hail Marys, and Bob's your uncle! The Promised Land is back within reach!

On one particular Sunday, I played *Praise and Blame*, the new album from Tom Jones. Yes, the "What's New, Pussycat" playboy, he of tight genie-pants and silk shirts open to the waist, has had his libido dipped in the healing waters of the baptismal font!

The album is a journey through the dry-rotted Baptist churches of the Deep South, where the humid air is thick with sin and redemption. It's a fascinating and winning experiment and Jones is still in command of his legendary voice, making such selections as the Led Zeppelin chestnut "Nobody's Fault But Mine" sound like a heartfelt, bluesy confession.

Listening to Tom Jones get all holy on me makes me feel even worse for the sinful, reckless, and feckless behavior I displayed at a TJ show I attended.

It was a cold evening in Atlantic City, a frigid and salty wind whipping off the ocean as I held onto the boardwalk's handrail. I swayed with the breeze and things got fuzzy as I stumbled into the House of Blues, my big belly sloshing with beer and whiskey chasers at every step.

My friends have been raving about TJ's shows for years but I couldn't get past the cheesy 1970s playboy imagery in my mind to take him very seriously. On this tour, he was backed by Wyclef Jean of The Fugees, which piqued my interest. I finally caved, but not before numbing myself with alcohol in the likely occasion that he sucked.

Boy, was I wrong! Wyclef brought the funk that night and TJ chewed up the scenery onstage with a booming, playful voice and an intoxicating charisma—he believed every word he sang and so did I! He so inspired the ladies in the room that one by one, thin pink Y-shaped panties and the odd room key rained on the stage as TJ swiveled his hips and put the sex in sexagenarian!

The funk. The sweat. The passion. The booze! I was completely under his spell and swept up in the sexually charged magic of the night! My drunken logic inspired me to cry aloud to no one in particular: "Why should the ladies have all the fun?"

In the heat of the moment, I stumbled into a bathroom stall, dropped my trousers, wiggled out of my boxer briefs, and zipped up again. Commando Mike was in the house and stumbling toward the stage, rudely plowing over everyone in my path with my considerable girth!

"Love is like candy on a shelf/ You want to taste and help yourself/ The sweetest things are there for you/ Help yourself take a few/That's what I want you to do," he sang during his campy hit, "Help Yourself." Despite my valiant efforts, I was only able to get within 10 feet of him. I crumpled my underwear into a ball and vaulted it toward the microphone stand. The abundance of cloth needed to cover my distended belly and posterior broke open from its bundle, my underwear transforming into a billowy ship mast in the shadow of the dusty spotlight as it headed for TJ. He saw it coming, his expression froze, and he tucked his chin into his chest before diving for cover in the mic stand.

"Whoa!" he exclaimed, breaking character dramatically right before he shrugged and flashed a megawatt smile. "Fans come in every shape and size, and that was a big one!"

I lost a pair of underwear that night but Sir Tom Jones gained a fan for life. I now "praise" his talent and "blame" myself for being a hot, drunken mess. Will you grant me redemption, Sir Tom?

A "Destiny" with Teen Angst

I just unpacked the last bag from the school band trip down in Wildwood, New Jersey. You'd have thought I was going to the Garden of Gethsemane for a pre-crucifixion from the way I carried on to my wife last Friday about the long car ride alone with a gaggle of girls, the crush of crowds in the sweltering sun around the parade route, and the boring band parents in this communal adventure with whom I shared little in common.

That belly-aching came to a screeching halt and a lump rushed to my throat as I watched my stunningly beautiful eighth- grader board the school bus to the parade route with her clarinet and sheet music for the last time. Another milestone in her life was whizzing by me way too fast, and I decided then and there to halt my complaining and enjoy the moment before it escaped me.

After the long march, the parents treated the girls to pizza and all the rides they could stomach on the expansive boardwalk. Each parent had just shelled out $48 apiece for the "all-u-can-ride" wrist band and against her better judgment, my Annie gave me a nervous peck on the cheek and whispered a rapid-fire "thanksIloveyoudad" before her friends could see it. We went to the first ride, an imposing bungee-jump contraption, and were informed that this would cost an additional $15!

"I can't believe you're ruining my last band weekend by not letting me go on this," screeched one of the girls in our party to her mother.

"Really, Mom? I can't go on? Really?" hissed another, stamping her feet for emphasis.

Back in the day, this kind of behavior would have earned me what my dad described as "a clitter on the gob." I said a silent prayer of thanks to my Maker that my daughter was raised better than that and for the Continental Airlines customer service representative who instilled in me the lessons on how to deal with a whiner.

Dig if you will the picture: I have just been unceremoniously dumped out of a plane in Newark, body and soul weary from a five-hour delay in Cleveland. The skies spewed everything they had at our propeller plane, inspiring me to reach for the barf bag more than once. My blood percolated when the baggage carousel stopped without giving up my luggage and I was in such a rage that I don't remember stomping over to the customer service counter for my date with Destiny, an expansive black woman clad in a blue flight-attendant suit two sizes too small.

I repeated the above paragraph to her, only I laced it with profane language and in my "outside voice." She sat back, chewed on the inside of her cheek for a moment, and nodded appreciatively until I had no more bile to spill on her face.

"You done?" she asked gamely.

"I guess," I shouted back.

"Well, there's 2 of us that give a shit about your bags right about now and one of us is losing interest real quick," she replied in a calm, icy tone. Butter would not melt in this woman's mouth as she cleared her throat. "So, why don't you take five steps back, think for a few moments about the tone of voice that might best convince me to help get your bags back, and then come back to the counter and we'll start this joyride all over again. Ya think ya can do that, sugar?"

I learned then and there that it is difficult to walk backward when your tail is between your legs. It also taught me a valuable lesson in raising teenage girls: nothing good can come from matching their hormonal drama with melodrama.

"There's two of us who care about you going on that $15 ride and one of us is starting to lose interest really quick" would have been an ideal response for these mothers as they defused the teenage hormonal bomb ticking on the boardwalk. My two girls have heard a variation of this sentence applied to so many situations that they don't even bother pulling that malarkey on me any longer.

"Oh, brother," my daughter said aloud, rolling her eyes. "It's just a ride and there are tons of other ones on this boardwalk. Let's just go on something else!"

The gaggle of girls flounced behind her as they lined up for a roller coaster and the two mothers stared at me with their mouths open. On a weekend wherein I suffered through bum notes on the tuba and missed cues from the drum corps, I relished this moment. My daughter's words were sweet music to her dad.

How Did We Come to This?

I had business in Newark one day and happened upon a copy of *The Jersey Journal,* the newspaper I delivered as a child but upon which I hadn't laid eyes in decades. The news of the murder of Leiby Kletzky, an 8-year-old Orthodox Jewish boy whose remains were found in the killer's refrigerator and a nearby trash bin, was dropped on the front page like a tray of drinks.

The story was so horrific that it was necessary to take breaks between paragraphs, for every detail is exactly as your worst parental nightmares can imagine. You cry along with the live coverage of the rabbi's bullhorn speech outside the temple that night, his voice breaking as he struggles to come to grips with savagery so deep it makes one question the very existence of God.

I was around Leiby's age when I started delivering the *Journal* through the streets etched in the hillside of Jersey City Heights. My bike was wobbly under the weight of the papers as I would fling the latest news onto the doorstep by day and then knock on that same door in the evenings to collect the money for the weekly delivery.

I was invited into countless houses as customers fumbled in their purses or wallets for cash. You think how many times you could have met the same fate as poor Leiby as adults lured you into the parlor and you say a silent prayer in thanks that God kept you safe years ago.

I'm sure newspaper organizations are keenly aware of the liabilities and risks of putting a child in that situation nowadays, which is why they now go the impersonal route of paper route management and bill customers online for home delivery. Paper routes cover entire towns as ever fewer people get their news from tree pulp and if you put my paper carrier in a lineup and ask me to pick that person out, I couldn't do it.

You think of the neighborhood you were brought up in and how it so mirrors Leiby's environment. There is a tight-knit community of Orthodox Jews in his Brooklyn neighborhood who stick to themselves while the outside world gawks at their black clothes, long beards, and stovepipe hats. The notion that his murderer emerged from that same community is simply incomprehensible.

In the 1970s of my youth, Hudson County might as well have been another county of Ireland, with so many of the "folks from home" occupying the shingled working-class houses. The racist inclination in the phrase "those people" referred to the Polish Catholics and Italian Catholics that somehow snuck into your little Irish-American enclave. How's that for diversity?

I often wondered as a child what ran through my parents' mind as they looked out the back window of our apartment; the lush patchwork fields and majestic mountains of Ireland replaced by a rust-dusted industrial landscape dotted with factories and semi trucks instead of lambs. The Irish huddled tightly with one another in this new land and everyone watched over the community's children, probably because they were all joined by their lonesomeness for home.

One of my earliest memories was being parked on the street of Central Avenue alongside other strollers as my parents joined other moms and dads for some shopping in Rosen's Furniture showroom.

How did we get here? Parents never had to worry about parking the stroller on the busy street with nothing more than a milk bottle in the child's hands. Now, your eyes dart nervously over to the car every few seconds when you chance leaving the kids while you take a few steps into the 7-Eleven for a carton of milk and even then, you wonder if some Child Services van will screech into the parking lot and slap cuffs on you.

It's fashionable to say the world is a different place now and you can't trust anyone anymore, but I'm not buying that entirely. Creeps, pedophiles and murderers didn't just show up in the last decade. Let's tell a nasty truth: we just made it easier for them to operate.

Despite the inner-city dynamic, parents knew every kid in a two-block radius when and where I grew up, and they also knew faces and models of cars that didn't belong on the street. Today, in my Shore neighborhood, there is a whole row of houses at the lip of my cul de sac and I couldn't tell you any last names of the inhabitants.

A community kept the kids in line and if Mrs. Rossi yelled at you, your parents didn't instantly pitch a fit and take the kid's side of the argument as they do now.

We didn't have iPods plugged into our ears at all times. A rapist could be pillaging victims at will in the woods where I walk my dog at night and I would never hear it because of the loud music that drums through my headphones.

Security cameras clearly caught poor Leiby Kletzky walking by himself, confused as to the right direction home before grainy video shows him entering a car for a ride that soon ends his life. Your heart breaks for the family as everyone became a mourner the night he died and the larger community wept on the humid sidewalk. Times have indeed changed and so have you. You'd like to think you come from good Irish stock and are not so detached from your fellow man that you wouldn't notice a confused little boy wandering the sidewalk, but you soon lose confidence that your presence would have made a difference on a Brooklyn street this week.

I pray for the boy's innocent soul and for the parents' solace. I add another prayer to become a better citizen in my community. Perhaps that's the message and call to action that our Maker sends to us all with this tragic death, and those like it. Rest in peace, Leiby.

Off Kilter

I always turn up my nose at the made-in-China plastic green nonsense that they peddle at an Irish festival. Rather, I favor rewarding unique Irish craftsmanship with my hard-earned cash. When I was at the Dublin Irish Festival in Ohio, I was amazed by the number of punk rockers wearing the AmeriKilt.

As the name implies, this Pennsylvania company has modernized the traditional Scottish garment. Gone are the tartan patterns that broaden the size of your ass to the naked eye. In this model, the kilts come in colors you'd find at The Gap and they have a number of pockets to accommodate your gadgetry. Ingenious! The owner couldn't have been nicer as I shook his hand and we arrived at a price.

I ditched my board shorts on the spot and began my strut across the fairgrounds. I had heard that wearing a kilt gave new appreciation to the term "stiff breeze," but wind was in short supply on this midsummer night. The thick, soupy air made everything hang a bit lower under the kilt—I mean, as low as an Irishman can go and you don't have to remind me that it's not very low by some standards.

I made the mistake of drinking beer by the barrel and before long, I found myself at the trough in a wheeled bathroom trailer. I dropped my boxer briefs at the knees, lifted my new kilt, and began to relieve myself when a Scotsman wearing a tartan model came up beside me.

He wasn't so much a man as he was a grill of an 18-wheeler with a watermelon for a head impaled on the hood ornament. His face was tomato red and his shirt was wet against his back after a round of Highland games. He towered over me and looked down as I balanced myself.

"That's not underwear under that kilt, is it?" he snorted.

"Yeah, it's my first time wearing one of these things."

"That's a nice vagina, luv. I can see it from here," came the reply.

After a shiver and a shake, he finished up before I did and slapped me on the back as he left the trailer. With that, I made the decision to go commando if I was going to do this at all. I dropped my underwear on the floor and kicked it into a garbage can.

Within minutes, my thighs began to burn as they rubbed against each other (as well as other things not suitable to mention in these pages). Soon I was in such agony that when I spotted a white bottle of baby powder next to a woman changing her toddler's diaper on the lawn, I thought I was seeing a mirage!

I crouched, straightened my back, and rocked back and forth with each step I took in a feeble attempt to separate my thighs. It was no use. It felt like I was peeling a layer of skin with each step. I quickly waddled over to her like an emperor penguin and asked—no, scratch that, I *pleaded*—for a few handfuls of that powder. I cupped two mounds in my hand and gingerly stepped over to the bathroom, and let's just say the cloud of white smoke you saw coming out of the port-a-john did not indicate the election of a new pope!

This provided huge relief, and I regained both my composure and strut once more. Alas, the night became more humid and before long, the powder became a thick paste that was no match for the relentless friction. By the time I reached the car, the heat underneath had cooked so much of the batter lining my legs that I was dropping funnel-cake flakes out from under the kilt with each step.

I know the Scots get their knickers in a twist when you refer to a kilt as a skirt, but let's be real. When you pull into a CVS wearing one and you are standing in the checkout line with a tube of Monistat Soothing Care Chafing Relief Powder-Gel at 2 AM, you can't help but think that it is the most emasculating moment of your life.

I tore open the package with my teeth and lay on the hotel bed naked with my legs spread and applied the cream under the kilt. By now, my lower half is an angry red hue with more bumps than a page of Braille.

I was feeling a bit better after applying the Monistat on the second day. Walking was not as painful and the breeze delivered on the kilt's promise of more chills and thrills, so to speak. I had regained my mojo!

Fortified by this new confidence, I took the risky step of leaving the comfort of the festival grounds, where everyone was wearing a kilt, and running through airport security, where no one else was wearing one.

I was thinking of a quote I recently read in Glenn O'Brien's brilliant new book, *How to Be a Man: A Guide to Style and Behavior for the Modern Gentleman.*

"Who looks stupid? The wallflower who just sits there, afraid of action, or the guy who's good to go, even if sometimes half-cocked? The man of action might make a mistake, but sometimes it's better to do it wrong than do nothing at all. Even if a man of action screws up, it's harder to notice because his velocity makes him a little blurry."

I found that when I was self-conscious about walking around in a kilt, trying to be as blurry as possible, the heat of mocking eyes staring at me proved too much to bear.

In times like this, you have to ask yourself, what would Gaga do? I found that out when I stared down a guy with a look on my face that said, *Where's your sense of style, bitch?* the kilt made sense. A flirty young cashier who whistled, winked and said, "Nice legs, bro...rock that kilt!" didn't hurt, either! Lady Gaga on her new album sings, "I'm on the right track, baby, I was born this way!" Indeed.

It's the last gasp of summer and time is running out for you to make a statement. Let more insecure men have their board shorts, which cover everything above the knee. Scoff at the Eurotrash freaks who parade around in their Speedo banana hammocks. If a bully kicks sand in your face, you can moon him right back without having to drop your drawers! Lift up the kilt and tell him what he, and anyone else who thinks you look funny in a kilt, can kiss!

If you want to be an Irish man of style, the kilt is the only way to go on the beach! It takes a tough man to wear a kilt. If you think you have what it takes, log onto AmeriKilt.com.

Dial 911 for a Zero

As my daughter prepares for Confirmation and her final year of religious-education classes in grammar school, we find ourselves scrambling for community service hours as part of her curriculum. It took me back to a time when I was frantically trying to meet my quota for a similar class in my freshman year of high school.

My need for community service hours and an obsession with comic books led me to apply to the Monroe Township First Aid Squad as a cadet. I can recall a quote I gave to the local newspaper reporter when he covered the fledgling cadet program. "I like the idea of upsetting the balance between life and death by helping people in an emergency." The reporter nodded admiringly as he scribbled the line.

I didn't have the heart to tell him that I cut and pasted that line from an exchange between Robin and Commissioner Gordon in a DC Comics story I had just read, which had the top cop asking the Boy Wonder about the meaning of his life's work during some idle water cooler talk around the Bat Signal.

I passed the CPR class and was enrolled in a series of courses centering on basic first aid. I was taking these courses with Lisa (not her real name), a plain, plump girl with thick bifocals who looked like the love child of Velma from Scooby Doo and Peppermint Patty from the Peanuts gang. She was observant with a sharp tongue and a wickedly droll sense of humor, so we bonded immediately.

She was the daughter of a captain from a neighboring squad. At 15, we were the youngest cadets in the room. We had an easy yet sarcastic rapport because we were teenagers who of course knew more than anyone in the room, including our instructors.

On the last week of our course, we were told we were going to view a video of childbirth in an attempt to prepare us to receive a bundle of joy if the mother couldn't get to the hospital. I couldn't believe my luck! I had only seen a naked pygmy woman inside the glossy spread of the dog-eared *National Geographic* nestled between my box spring and mattress. Now, I could view a woman's body in the buff and get high school credits for it!

The room darkened and the reel tape clicked to life. I barely had time to focus on the pink, hairy patch of the promised land between her legs before it transformed into a spitting veal parmesan dinner. The more blood that was on the screen, the less of it seemed to make its way to my head. My salivary glands were bone-dry and I felt wobbly as I got up to compose myself in the bathroom.

"You OK?" asked Lisa as I returned to the folding chair next to hers.

I nodded bravely.

"This was pretty intense," she continued. "Hey, I've got an idea to clear our heads! I just got a bunch of new Atari video games for my birthday. Wanna come over and play them with me?" I nodded and we bicycled over to her house a mile away.

"Anybody home?" she shouted as we entered the house. An absent-minded grunt from an older brother could be heard from the living room. We ran through the hall to her bedroom and turned on the television and the gaming console.

I was well on my way to doubling her score at Asteroids when she asked to see my joystick.

"You have your own," I grumbled.

She put her hand between my legs.

"I don't have one of these," she cooed.

Before I could ask her what the hell she was doing, the door of her room burst open and her father flicked on the light. Lisa scrambled to her feet and it was then I noticed that only a thin, raggedy pair of tight pink panties with a brown racing stripe up the middle was covering her fleshy ass. For the second time in an hour, the blood left my head.

Her father, a small but surprisingly strong and agile man, grabbed my wrist and flung me toward the door. I was rabbit-hopping down the stairs when I saw Lisa's enormous brother blocking the front door.

The threat of having my parents called was the only thing keeping me on the front porch of their double-wide trailer as her father laid into me with a lecture he'd probably had in his back pocket since his only daughter was in kindergarten. I was told all about the sins of the flesh, complete with biblical chapters and verses. It was clear he was a militant Protestant who had his Bible down cold, presenting another clear disadvantage for me in this situation. My family, like most Catholics, never actually read the Bible as a leisure activity—we let others read it and then took their word for it when they threw around the quotes and references.

"After seeing the video you just saw, I can't believe you'd be so stupid as to engage in premarital sex with my daughter."

"But…"

"Shut up!" he shouted before gagging on a mouthful of mustard-colored chewing tobacco that was swirling inside his mouth as he spoke.

"You got the wrong guy, sir," I said. "We're just friends."

"I was born at night but I wasn't born last night, son," he replied, spitting a gob of tobacco sludge into the unkempt grass for emphasis. "You two sure looked cozy in that bedroom with her skirt off and all."

"Sir, she's a nice girl but she's not my type," I said. "I just came to play a video game. I have no interest in her."

"Why?"

"Because you guys have the new Asteroids game here and I had never played it."

"Jesus, you're dumber than you look. I meant why isn't she your type? You calling my little girl ugly?"

"N-n-no," I stammered when all I wanted to say was "y-y-yes!" *No amount of community service hours would be worth tapping that charity case*, I thought.

With my tombstone teeth held back with mesh wiring underneath a bowl haircut and above a wanton pale gut, I was certainly no prize.

Still, I wasn't *that* desperate.

"I think we got off on the wrong foot, sir. I didn't mean any disrespect in your house or with your daughter. May I please go?"

I pedaled home, convinced that my mother would have gotten the call by the time I got there. There was no mention of it as I wheeled my bike into our garage and washed up for supper. Ol' Mike had lived to fight another day, but it wasn't long before I would regret that, too.

On the following morning, I was given a police scanner and a few white uniforms. Like a superhero, I had my costume and a lo-fi version of the Bat Signal! I sat there on the edge of my bed for hours, jumping each time the scanner crackled to life and the dispatcher shot the bull with the patrol cars circling our town.

I didn't have to wait long for action. A piercing siren in the woods near our house would alert the whole neighborhood that there was an emergency and the police scanner would give the details. I would pedal my bike at top speed over to the squad building, making it just in time to hop into the waiting ambulance.

The comic books dealt with life and death situations all the time, but they never actually described what life and death looked and felt like. There were never any pools of blood around dead bodies. There might be a trickle of red stuff coming out of Batman's nose if the Joker pimp-slapped him too hard; that was about it.

I had to push the Grim Reaper out of the doorway right after the rig pulled into one of the bays at a nursing home. An old man's breathing was extremely labored when we got inside his cramped room. We slipped the flimsy clear buttercup mask over his ears and let the oxygen flow into him as we loaded him onto the gurney. By the time we had loaded him into the back of the ambulance, his heart had stopped. The captain began chest compressions on the gurney for a few minutes and then felt his hand for a pulse. Nothing. She made the Sign of the Cross and I followed her lead. She looked at her watch and made notes on the time of death in our log.

Driving to the hospital in these tight quarters, with a dead body rolling toward me on the gurney with each bump in the road, wigged me right out for the rest of the night.

Any trauma I had from the night before became a distant memory the next morning when the police scanner announced that the woman around the block from me was going into labor. I knew the address from my paper route, and their house was closer than the squad building, so I slipped into my one-piece white jumpsuit and pedaled over to their house. The rig skidded into the driveway as my kickstand hit the pavement.

The shrill cries I heard inside the house are ones that will stay with me until I draw my last breath. There was a flurry of activity in the hallway as the father-to-be stuffed his wife's belongings into a duffel bag while we lifted her gurney until the wheels below locked in place.

"What in the name of God is our paperboy doing here?" she said as her eyes widened, her face turned red, and she lunged for my hand when a contraction gripped her. She could have crushed the bones of my fingers with her grip. In the unfolding excitement, I completely forgot anything I learned in training the week before. This would happen again 25 years later as my wife pushed through the pain while I scrambled to remember what my Lamaze classes had taught me. But I digress!

The ride to the hospital was 10 minutes but it felt like an hour; she cursed a blue streak at her husband for doing this to her when she wasn't howling in agony.

My nervous bladder quickly filled amidst the drama and soon ached with each bounce of the rig; I completely pissed myself within a block of the hospital bay. Luckily, the woman's water broke and sprayed the gurney at around the same time and I was able to blame my wetness on that.

The ambulance dropped me back at the woman's house and I pedaled home, dejected and defeated. I washed my soiled uniform, packed it in a box with the police scanner, and pedaled over to the squad building.

My stint as a kid superhero was over, making the town safe to be saved by someone else. Now, if I could have just found a way to get community service hours for that act of mercy....

Too Fat for Toro

I am in the middle of reading *Tough Sh*t,* the hilarious rags-to-riches motivational book by Jersey filmmaker Kevin *(Clerks)* Smith. One chapter recalls his unfortunate run-in and subsequent Twitter war with Southwest Airlines in 2010, which was picked up by every news outlet at the time.

You might recall that Smith, a self-described "sedentary processed-foods consumer," was asked to leave his airline seat when a flight attendant deemed his presence on the flight to be a safety issue because the armrests of his seat might not be able to come down for the passenger next to him. That was a polite way of saying he was too fat to fly.

Anyone carrying weight could feel his pain, but I perhaps had a greater empathy because something similar happened to me later that summer.

Let's call out the elephant in the room before we go any further: me.

Yes, I have weight to lose. I'm fat. There, I've said it. For the last few decades, I am flirting slightly above the National Institutes of Health's "morbidly obese" classification but well below the need to have an EMT crew cut bricks from the side of the house to get me to a doctor's appointment.

In some circles, I am a god that would give Brad Pitt a run for his money. My gay friends call me a "bear," a hefty, hairy man who attracts thinner and hotter "cubs" in their community. If only that same dynamic existed in the hetero world!

I've never needed a second seat or even a seatbelt extender on any flight I've ever been on; I acknowledge this milestone would be proof-positive of a failed exercise regimen should it ever come to pass.

My incident happened during a sweltering summer day at Six Flags Great Adventure in Jackson, New Jersey. I had just endured a tortuous wait in a long line with my daughter Annie at the entrance of the El Toro roller coaster ride. We waited a bit longer than we should have and let the next coaster go so that we could sit in the front seat on the next ride. We approached the coaster and were asked to slide into the last seats on our right. A harness above us hissed and a steel bar coated in foam descended onto our shoulders, because this ride involved going upside down and defying gravity in other ways.

An alarm sounded as everyone settled into their seats for a ride. "Seat 1A's harness is not secured," came the announcement on the loudspeaker. A pair of teenagers approached our row.

"Sir, you need a little help with that?" asked one of the boys.

"It seems like it clicked to me," I offered weakly. My daughter smiled nervously.

One of the boys lifted the harness up and then slammed it down on my belly, meeting resistance right before it had the opportunity to click into the seatbelt-like apparatus between my legs.

"This. Won't. Go. Down," he grunted.

"So. Close!" groaned the other as he put his weight down on the harness. My legs became numb as the safety bar cut off the circulation into my upper thighs.

There was a murmur of riders wondering why we weren't moving yet that was clearly audible behind me.

"I'm sorry, sir," announced one of the boys. "It's not safe for you to ride this coaster."
I turned to my daughter, got assurance from her that she would be able to ride the coaster by herself, and extricated myself from the seat.

"Poor Dad," said Annie. It was meant to be comforting. It wasn't. Even more uncomfortable was the walk of shame past everyone else on the ride, their judging eyes on the Irish-American hippopotamus that waddled toward the exit row.

I was greeted by a fleshy black rapper whose gold chains jingled as he gave the ride operators a middle-finger salute.

"You discriminated against me and my boy here 'cos we was fat," he said, grabbing me by the shoulder. "In front of our muthafuckin' kids! That shit's cold!"

"Fuck 'em," I whispered in his ear. "It's not worth it."

"Da hail it ain't!" he screamed. "This shit ain't over. This shit ain't ovahhh!"

The operators must have alerted security about this two-man tubby protest because a park representative greeted us at the bottom of the exit ramp. There was a security detail sitting in a golf cart nearby in case things got out of hand.

"We are sorry that happened," she said cautiously. "I'm sure you can understand how the safety of our guests is Priority One here at Six Flags."
"Yeah. My ass!" said my black beluga brother-in-arms.

"I understand," I replied, making sure I sidestepped away from him. "I'm cool. A little embarrassed, but cool."

She bit her lip sympathetically.

"I can't imagine."

Yeah, lady, you can't. She was 90 pounds soaking wet and we looked like the number 10 standing next to each another.

"I'd like to offer a free meal for you and your family. Have a treat on us!"

I took the coupons and smiled meekly as my daughter bounced down the ramp and threw her arms around me in a show of support.

Once again, I had a hole in my ego and self-esteem that only a gob full of churros and nachos could fill and we set off to do just that with our free food coupons.

A Learned Eejit

No more pencils

No more books

No more teacher's dirty looks

Out for summer

Out till fall

We might not go back at all

Those are the lyrics from Alice Cooper's classic song "School's Out," and I'm singing them with gusto at the very time my kids are preparing to go back to school.

Yes, at the tender age of 45, I put an end to an academic career and let's just say Albert Einstein never had to look over his shoulder. After three long years, I attained my master's degree in management. While I'm proud to say I graduated summa cum laude, 'tis a far cry from my "summa cum lucky" nightmare that was my undergraduate study!

After the last week of class, my parents came over for Sunday dinner. We have a tradition in my house of putting great grades on the refrigerator and my academic achievement was no exception! My dad looked at the grades and nodded approvingly. "'Tis a credit to yeh, really," the Athenry native said over his bifocals. "Really, really nice work."

He turned and handed me a small gift bag. "We got yeh a little something for the occasion," he said. "Oh, there's a T-shirt that we got yeh for Father's Day that we forgot to throw in the bag last time, so that's in there, too."

After opening an envelope with a gift card to my favorite boutique, I unrolled a kelly-green T-shirt from the bag. On it was one word in big, black letters: EEJIT. Of course, this is the Irish slang for the word *idiot*.

I laughed out loud when I first saw my father wearing it a few weeks ago after he came home from a weekend Irish festival. I had given him a right tongue-lashing for not thinking to buy one for his son.

Was this his way of making up for his mistake? Perhaps, but I can't help but think the timing of this gift, at the same time as my graduation with an advanced degree, was a little suspect. Coincidence? I think not.

If you don't know what I'm on about by now you probably weren't raised by real Irish parents the way I was. Giving me a T-shirt that said "eejit" sent a message home: there's not much difference between a feckin' eejit and a learned eejit when you come right down to it. And nothing is worse than an eejit who puts on airs and thinks he's the cock on the walk with his new degree!

Sure, my parents were intensely proud that their son achieved an education well beyond theirs and most of the family. Indeed, this was the fulfillment of an immigrant's dream, wasn't it? You made sacrifices so that your kids got farther up the ladder in the new land than you ever would. Indeed, it wouldn't be an exaggeration to think that this accomplishment was just as much theirs as it was mine.

Still, you don't get carried away with yourself. Gloating on Facebook and carrying on about how great you are is akin to an Amish boy discovered behind the wheel of a 1984 Camaro by his pastor: *you will be shunned if you keep that up*.

Even though I have my master's, I am not through learning from my parents. Saying everything by saying nothing at all is an art form. Opening a care package from home in my dorm and finding a local Mass bulletin and Confession schedule taped to the baked goods. Placing a girlie magazine on the pillow when the stash was found whilst flipping the mattress. These are all examples of the silent guidance that kept me on the straight and narrow during my teenage years and I reflect on the brilliant, not-so-subtle messaging this week as I sit through a new student orientation at my elder daughter's high school.

My mom and dad may not have a master's degree, but they raised a learned eejit who believes they are well deserving of an honorary doctorate in parenting with a minor in handling a teenager!

Back to School Is No Longer "Tough"

Like so many dads, I find myself this past Sunday in an outlet mall with my elbows hooked around the back of a bench while my girls diminish my net wealth by the millisecond. There's a heightened sense of urgency around back-to-school shopping this year for three reasons: a hurricane wiped out a whole week of buying, the first day of autumn came early and ushered in a chill that invalidated our shorts, and one daughter is obsessed with getting her look right as she steps into high school for the first time.

As they ping-pong between stores and the bags at my feet pile up, I can't help but be envious at the choices they have at this age. Both girls are zaftig, just like their mom and dad were in their teens. Unlike them, I didn't have much decision in clothes at a time I needed it the most.

Back in the 1970s we certainly didn't benefit from the proliferation of cheap Chinese clothing or sympathetic designers that catered to plus-sized teens. Then there was the small matter of budget: any extra money Mom and Dad had when I was growing up either got sent home to their parents in Ireland or toward a fund to spring us from the cramped two-family house in Jersey City and into the suburbs.

An irregularly shaped guy like me had two choices: the hand-me-downs from my older cousin Robert, or the "husky" section of Sears. Like my brother, Brendan, Rob had a wiry, athletic build, so my brother usually benefited from Rob's clothes pile.

Vertigo was the best way to describe the dizzying effect the loud checkered patterns had when stacked on the racks at Sears. The Toughskin jean was the fabric of choice for your favorite fatty, according to the sadistic designers who thought putting noisy patterns on a wide rump would look attractive.

I remember how well Sears touted the new line of Toughskins children's pants as "the toughest of Sears' tough jeans...lab tests prove it!" The pants were manufactured with a blend of materials, including Dacron Type 59 polyester, DuPont 420 nylon, and cotton. If the cotton part makes you think the fabric was breathable, think again. And good luck trying to bend your knees in them the first few months after purchase!

To demonstrate just how tough the new jeans were, Sears launched a famous "Tough Jeans Territory" ad campaign in 1974, in which the department store constructed a trampoline out of the Toughskin material. Sears was so sure of the new line of pants that they were sold with a guarantee that children would grow out of their Toughskin jeans before the jeans wore out!

That was all my mother had to see. Durability was the most important feature for my mom because there wasn't a lot of money to spend and the chore of trying to shoe-horn my flab into new back-to-school gear was the kind of torture she would endure but once a year.

Altering this tough fabric was impossible. Mom would either slice the fabric with industrial sewing scissors that left a jagged edge of a hem or she'd make a cuff by rolling the seam away from my shoelaces.

Through countless years of continuous overtime work at the New Jersey Turnpike, my father had finally saved enough to move one summer, and when I stepped into my new suburban school that September, I was a sight to behold.

Two wires strained to pull the tombstone buck teeth back into a mouth that was situated below a bowl haircut and just above the pillowy double chin. My pale flesh spilled like an albino muffin top over the unforgiving fabric, which resisted the flab avalanche with the aid of a thick white belt. Of course, I was the laughingstock of the school while my brother assimilated easily by scoring countless goals with the soccer team.

I took a job with a lawn service one summer and lost weight, which helped me fit in. Today, I just try to fit into a plane seat because I now look like the thin lawn boy Mike if he had taken on water-bloat after his lifeless body was dredged from the bottom of a lake.

"I saw some nice shirts in there," my wife said sportingly, glancing over to the Guess outlet. I know better than to waste the energy to move from the bench. I know Guess makes those "slim fit" shirts that have no tolerance for stomachs like mine. If they come up with a "husky" section, maybe they'll get my business during the next back-to-school season.

A Frank Discussion About Neighbors

When your cul de sac has this many older folks on it, your mind goes to the worst-case scenario each time an ambulance blocks your driveway, as it did this morning. Your heart sinks as you watch the worried and bewildered wife scurry in the direction of the gurney that was raised into the back of the rig. Your throat lumps up when she returns as a widow hours later, eyes puffy. Our block is quiet and feels empty without our good friend and neighbor, Frank Veltre.

Frank was the custodian of our local school for decades and though he may have retired a while back, he was the kind of guy with energy to burn and was always working with his hands. Even at 76, he was always up on a ladder or tending to the immaculate flower beds on his small patch of greenery. You wouldn't be long on your lawn putting patio furniture together before he'd shoot over with a toolbox to lend a helping hand. That's just the kind of guy Frank was.

Being retired, he had nothing but time to talk to you when you pulled into the driveway. This leisurely relationship with the clock was often at odds with the hectic schedule of the parent/ taxi driver/on-the-go writer and businessman. Truth be told, there were times I either didn't have time or was not in the mood for conversation. Frank would often approach the driveway when I pulled in and I'd smile gently, pointing to the wireless headset in the ear when I was on a call. When time was especially tight, I'd put the thing in my ear when I was rounding the block, just to avoid conversation. Before long, he wouldn't even bother coming over; he'd just wave from a distance and ask about the family. I'm left with a deep sense of regret and shame about that.

It's certainly a far cry from how neighbors interact with one another in Athenry, County Galway, where my dad grew up. As we left Uncle Mattie's house and walked down the hill to Granny Farragher's a few houses away, we'd always meet a few cars ambling up the busy street. Drivers would wave and nod, even if they didn't know you.

The citizens of rural Ballylanders were just as welcoming. I remember a postman delivering Granny Cleary's mail, who would smile when you told him who you were. "Yerra, amen't I the one that delivers those letters to yer granny from the Yanks every month? She always looks forward to those. Ye brighten herself's day," he would say before turning to Granny and discussing the gossip from every house along his route. Imagine a mail carrier doing that over here? He'd be sued for slander!

When my cousin Linda got married in Athenry, I was struck by this custom of bonfire lighting that the whole town seemed to turn out for. Turf and wood fires were lit in driveways as her limousine and motorcade snaked through the narrow boreens, neighbors waving enthusiastically as we waved back from the car. The dark turf smoke would lick the blackberry vines that clung to the stone walls across the street, creating a canopy of well wishes for the newly minted couple.

I also have fond memories of Granny Farragher pouring mugs of tea and tall glasses of orange soda without complaint as half the town would parade through her door to see Mick and his family from America. Michael John Rabbitte, the Costellos, Mary Furey, and a cast of lovely characters would recount stories from their youth while lamenting over those who had passed on. No matter how far away my father lived, he was always part of that community.

Some folks might say that this is the Ireland of yesteryear, with most younger folks retreating into their iPod earbuds the same way they do in America. I hope that's not the case. It's sad that we only get together in community nowadays when a terrorist attacks or when a flood turns us all out in the street. We claim to be connected to hundreds of people, yet we know deep down that a Facebook message here and there does not make you related to the people in your community. I should know better than that because it's especially inexcusable for a writer to keep the warm conversation of a neighbor at bay. Writers are supposed to be observant and curiously engaged with our fellow man as we scribble our take on life. When did I forget that?

I look over at the mound of flowers covering Frank's grave as I walk the dog today. I stop and say three prayers: one for his kind soul, one for answers on how to inject warm Irish hospitality into this neighborhood, and a third to ward off ambulances visiting our cul de sac for the foreseeable future.

Laughter Is NOT the Best Medicine

As the father of two sharp daughters, I should have known it would happen one of these days.

Longtime readers of my columns and blogs know that I often split the pulp and ink into two parts: one on the music news of the week and the other on funny anecdotes on my life and the keen-eyed, snarky observation about the weird tics of my family.

Well, I just got burned from that harsh light of observation.

I came downstairs from my home office and my girls erupted in laughter. I instantly checked my zipper, as most men do when confronted with a wall of giggles from the opposite sex.

"What's so funny?"

My oldest prodded my youngest to speak up.

"Okay, Dad, this is you painting," said Maura.

A wee bit of background: I had spent the last couple of days repairing the water-damaged ceiling of my girls' bathroom before painting the ceiling white and the walls a bright—and unforgiving—orange hue. I had painted on a bit of drama about how difficult the claustrophobic conditions were because I wanted to be left alone with my thoughts and my iPod.

She stood up as if taking a thespian's stage.

"For this trick, I'll need to curse," she said, looking my way. "Daddy, is that OK, just this once?"

I nodded cautiously. With that, she started simulating dragging a roller over the walls and imitated me singing my favorite Stones songs while painting. It went something like this:

"Brown Sugar! How come...oh, f**k meeee! I said yeah, yeah, yeah...dammit to hell!"

With that, hilarity ensued.

"I like when he does this," my oldest exclaimed, jumping out of her seat in her determination not to be upstaged by the younger sister.

She made her right hand into the shape of a gun and shot it, making a farting noise with each "click of the trigger." Thus, I deeply regretted my ritual announcing of the passing of gas around the house over the years. I also became present to my immense gratitude for the steel-hand-in-the-velvet-glove presence of my wife around the house as she takes the higher road in setting models of feminine decorum for my two girls to follow. Without her, my girls would make Honey Boo Boo Child look like Mary Poppins if all they had was a dad pointing them in the right direction with his "gas pistol."

Alas, writers must always get the last word. I said nothing, pointing instead to the refrigerator magnet that said, *Careful, or you'll be in my next novel* before going upstairs.

To my own parents, I say something a bit different when they get on my case: "Remember who is writing your eulogy."

It really works for me to have the last word! But on this day, as I slunk back to my upstairs office, a wave of terror overcame me. What if my girls decide to write a book about their old man one day? *This Is Your Brain on Shamrocks: The Next Generation?*

Yikes!

Let's Dance!

If you live long enough, you have moments wherein time has gone by so fast that you are now the parent supervising your children doing something that you feel like the kid version of you just did yesterday.

I was sitting in the expansive horseshoe driveway in front of the high school waiting for my daughter to emerge from her first homecoming dance. Wasn't it just yesterday that my father was sitting in an idling car waiting to pick up my friends from our high school dances?

On this night, fawnlike young girls with long, thin legs navigating high heels for the first time gingerly stepped past the span of my headlights and down the walkway. My daughter Annie approached the car, my headlights no match for her high-beam smile framed by the honey-kissed hair painstakingly straightened by an iron. There was confidence in her strut and once she got in the car, she recounted stories of politely rebuffing suitors and dancing with her girlfriends carefree. Man, was this a far cry from how I exited my high school dances!

I went to St. Joseph's High School in Metuchen, New Jersey. My wife, who was at those same dances prior to us actually meeting me in college a few years later, reports that the dances were huge draws for girls in the area because "St. Joe's was where all the hot guys with a future went."

This was true. This all-boy institution drew the cream of the crop academically and athletically from three surrounding counties. It was an extremely competitive environment, most noticeably when the boys jousted for the attention of the fairer sex at these dances.

To this day, I still wonder what a kid routinely picked last in gym class and with highly questionable study habits was doing in a mix like this, but there I was in an environment that totally amplified my teenage insecurities!

When you don't have the brains nor the brawn to bait the hook of love, you resort to desperate measures altogether: that fickle beast called fashion! The early 1980s saw the birth of MTV, and a barrage of its images were defining hot tastes at the time. David Lee Roth was encouraging you to "jump" on that channel but there was no way I could grow my hair that long without bearing the wrath of the Brothers of the Sacred Heart. Duran Duran trained us all on a "view to a kill," but I had to kill the idea of looking like them because the good Lord did not bless me with John Taylor's high cheekbones or Simon LeBon's lithe moves on the dance floor. Michael Jackson was quite a "thriller" to the ladies, but my skin wasn't dark enough. Of course, the King of Pop bleached his skin so many times that I actually became darker than him later in life, but that was no use to me at the time.

When I arrived at my first high school dance, I was a walking, talking meat grinder of MTV culture. Plus-sized gray plastic parachute pants that swished when you walked? Check. One white glove? Check. Red terrycloth headband wrapped around my oversized cabbage head to catch the "working for the weekend" look spawned by the fat dude in Loverboy? Check. Spiked hair with enough salon product to grease a wok? Check! White Capezio shoes with the real wood soles? Check. Ready for love? Check! Check! Check!

There was some Asian craze going on at the time, and I probably wore a T-shirt with Chinese lettering I didn't understand emblazoned across my chest and thick gut. If the translation didn't spell "hopeless douche," perhaps it should have.

Do I really need to tell you how the evening went? I hugged the wall like a vinca vine all night, looking forlorn as the swim studs and track stars swooped onto anything with a skirt. It was fortuitous that the red terrycloth number on my head came with matching wrist bands because they caught my tears as I watched my future wife do "The Safety Dance" with anyone else but me.

All's well that ends well in the dance of life. Even though the eventual love of my life was in the same room during that dreary high school sock hop and we never got a chance to slow-dance, I have been enjoying a passionate tango with her down the road of life today. Many of those jock types now fix my car and make my sub sandwiches. I know I shouldn't take pleasure in that, but God forgive me, I do. I wouldn't change things for the world today, but I sure wish I'd had the good sense to trade in those ridiculous MTV accessories for an ounce of my daughter's natural confidence and enthusiasm.

Girly Man o' the Gridiron

It's a typical Sunday in a typical living room on a typical winter day. The dinner plates are being cleared and it's not a moment too soon for the men around the table. Their eyes dart nervously between the wall clock and the black expanse of my flat-screen TV. With a permissive nod from one of the wives, they rush to the living room and fumble with the remote in time for some big football game to begin.

There I sit at the kitchen table, too manly to lift a finger in the direction of womenfolk and the dirty dish yet not feeling a testosterone rush from the cheers and jeers in the next room.

And so it goes pretty much every Sunday of my life. I never had interest in sports. I've watched a total of an hour of ESPN in my life, and even then, it was one of those gauzy documentaries about an injured athlete overcoming odds that moved me to tears. Heck, it might as well have aired on the Oxygen Network.

My lack of interest in sports has produced countless hours of uncomfortable pauses in conversation between myself and male co-workers over the years. I never get asked to join March Madness contests or football pools. I usually check my Blackberry or engage in some activity that has me look downward as the men around me swivel their necks from one screen to another when I'm out for an after-work drink at some sports bar. Anyone who has ever worked in an office with cubicles knows that the first 10 minutes of a Monday morning conference call is usually devoted to gridiron concerns.

After a while, it gets tedious and I stop the conversation by saying something like, "Uh, can someone tell me why the Green Bay Packers have yellow tights? I mean, they are GREEN Bay! Hellooo!"

Just calling a part of the uniform "tights," like it was a ballet or something, infuriates most diehard sports fans and the verbal assault on my manhood ensues. Deflecting a shortcoming with humor got me this far in life; why stop now?

On this particular evening, emotions run high around the television amongst the men in my family as the Giants wallop Green Bay. While all this was going on, I was curled up on the far side of our horseshoe-shaped sectional with my nose deep in *The New York Times*. I guess you could forgive me if I read the sports section to redeem myself, but I found Maureen Dowd's literary crucifixion of Newt Gingrich's campaign and the bitchy advice doled out by Philip Galanes in the Social Q column infinitely more interesting.

Now, in my defense, I don't watch much television of any kind. While most men assume quarterback position in their recliners and guzzle beer for hours at a time, I spend my Sundays writing books and columns. Except, of course, if there's a one-day sale at Macy's. Then I am the only straight guy at the mall on Super Bowl Sunday.

Then again, who can be sure of that? I know I am a red-blooded male deeply attracted to my luscious wife and the curves on a woman. Still, if a blaze consumed my home and they pried the DVR from my charred and dead hand, the fire marshal would use it as evidence that the owner of the house was a flaming queen that probably got tangled up in an equally flammable throw blanket. Sure, I could blame my wife and daughters with filling up the DVR memory banks to capacity with *Color Splash, House Hunters, Real Housewives of Beverly Hills, Toddlers and Tiaras, Hungry Girl, Say Yes to the Dress, RuPaul's Drag Race*, and *My Big Fat Gypsy Wedding*, but I'm a willing party who plops down on the couch whenever it's suggested we have a TV night as a family and it was me who bookmarked Lisa

Vanderpump's website on my browser.

I'm sure some lack of interest on my part comes from my less-than-stellar athletic career in school. I was a big boy all my life, which means I rocked the defensive end on a soccer field while my wiry brother ran up and down the field for glamorous goals. I was a decent enough soccer player locally, but my skills proved no match for the talent in the regional Catholic boys' high school that I attended. After one-too-many cuts from teams, I resigned myself to a life of being picked last in gym class and lost all appetite for organized sports.

But hey, if you want to take me out to the ball game, I'm down with that! Buy me some peanuts and Cracker Jacks! I don't care if I ever come back! Just don't ask me to regurgitate stats on the pitcher...he's the guy on the big mound in the middle of the field, right?

Comic Book Blues

Square jaws. Ripping six-pack abs contained under tight shirts. Good triumphing over evil. Is it any wonder that Hollywood has made a movie out of our comic book heroes. With escalating budgets and eye-popping special effects, Tinsel Town has brought our childhood fantasies to the big screen.

Most of the money I made on my paper route went straight to the comic book store on Central Avenue in Jersey City. I devoured the stories, mostly from the DC Comics stable of characters that included Batman, Robin, the Joker, and Superman. I remember the mad dash I'd be on after school on a Wednesday, when the new books would arrive at the store. I then re-created them with the many action figures that Santa brought me throughout the years. I remember watching in mock horror as the flimsy strings that held Aquaman's arms and legs together rotted out when you immersed him in the bathtub. In this case, water was not the friend of this King of Atlantis!

There was a lot more than childish games going on here—I'm quite sure the plot lines and staging of stories played out with the action figures shaped my storytelling just as much as Stephen King or Mary Higgins Clark did a bit later on.

Old habits die hard; I still find myself going to a little comic book shop near my office about once a month. My heart sank on one Wednesday when a "closed" sign hung on the door!

This doesn't necessarily mean the death of the comic book industry. According to Newsarama.com, an industry site, 2011 has leapt ahead of year-to-date 2010 sales by 5.47% in units and 1.87% in dollars.

Yet there's no denying how old the comic book shoppers are in any given shop these days. More kids will get their first taste of the Caped Crusader in the Batman: Arkham City video game than in a paper copy of the comic that bears his name. In fact, a DC Comics app allows you to download the new titles over the Internet each month, making a trip to the comic book store obsolete. Comic book retailers know this and are supplementing their income through merchandising candy, themed game cards, and expensive collectors' statuettes. DC Comics made a decision to publish comics with an iPad app, signaling yet another nail in the store concept.

The only people you see perusing the aisles of a comic book store these days are middle-aged men like me. These guys are characters unto themselves, and I don't mean the kind who wear a cape.

Check out that guy over there. He's the father of a Columbine kid in his long black trench coat. A Green Lantern logo is on an emerald T-shirt that is going to heroic lengths to hide the belly. His hair has been bleached with burnt-orange streaks and has been carefully manipulated to cover the thin patches on his scalp. The cashier is trying to politely keep up with the conversation in between customers but you get the sense he could care less about how "The New 52" re-launch hero campaign by DC Comics is a rip-off or how Batman should have taken care of the Dollmaker in two episodes, not four.

Next to him is a fan of Detective Comics who loves Paul Jenkin's storytelling about Commissioner Gordon and The Joker being held against their will. This guy is in a red hoodie with The Flash's lightning-bolt logo living large on his chest.

You wonder what would happen to these man-children if this shop closed down. Would they go back to searching for their virginity, which was last left under the seat cushion next to the cheese powder-encrusted Xbox joystick? What do those people do for work? They either live with their parents or they are multimillionaire computer game inventors—there's no in between.

It's easy to judge from where I sit now, at my desk. There's a Joker Pez dispenser amidst the cup of pens and I opened this morning's pile of bills using a black Bat letter opener with a stand that is emblazoned with the logo on Christian Bale's costume in the Dark Knight series. On the bookshelf on my left, in no particular order, are two Green Arrow action figures, a Spider-Man dangling from a piece of thread, a Justice League book stand, a Sandman bust, and a miniature version of every car Batman rode his Bat ass in.

I'm sure in the next 10 years, we will see an end to the comic book, and the dreams I have of cashing in the back issues that are carefully placed in plastic sleeves in my guest room closet will be dashed as middle-aged men like me lose interest in them. The younger generation of hero worshippers get their inspiration from a gaming console, and there's nothing in Batman's utility belt that can stop that.

What Is Irish?

I was ambling through County Clare en route to Athenry after landing at Shannon not long ago, and smiled at the sight of the familiar "welcome to Gort" sign that announces your entry into County Galway.

"That place is gone to us," said the driver. "It's just full of foreigners taking our jobs away from us."

Indeed, some 40 percent of the residents of Gort are non-Irish, according to the 2006 Census, and a majority of them are Brazilians. These people originally came to work in the meat-processing plants in Gort where the pay is generally much higher than in similar plants in Brazil.

I could smell a strong whiff of xenophobia in the pubs throughout my last short stay in Ireland. There was a loud cry of foul over how immigrants from either Poland and Algeria took jobs from the Irish and sucked on the Celtic Tiger boom years like vampire bats that drained their blood and then flew away when the cat got sick.

There was a high resentment of these outsiders intermingling with "the natives"—how it was delicately put—as if Ireland has its own thing going and we don't appreciate outsiders messing it up.

It makes one wonder if anything belongs to Ireland anymore? It brings the question: what makes something Irish in 2012? It could be debated that the land on the island itself is no longer theirs.

The self-inflicted banking crisis forced the Irish to swallow their pride and accept loans and bailout money from their neighbors to stay afloat. It's debatable as to who actually owns Ireland now. The Chinese? Germany? France?

It makes you want to take to the pub and have a good drink, but you won't find anything Irish in there to whet your whistle. Bushmills and Guinness are both owned by the Diageo Corporation, whose offices reside in downtown London. The lifeblood of Irish culture is owned by the Brits! Irish breakfast tea, or "tay" as they call it in the auld sod, is actually a blend of Assam tea leaves from the *camellia sinensis* plant that lines the Brahmaputra River in India!

Not even the Celtic Tiger was born in Ireland! American companies like Baxter, Microsoft, Boston Scientific, and IBM have been fueling the job growth in Ireland for decades, ever since Ireland aggressively marketed their highly educated natives and cut corporate tax rates. The influx of American companies makes the big cat that made Ireland roar more "Tony the Tiger" than Celtic Tiger.

Much of the stuff you buy in an Irish shop nowadays is made in China, especially the tchotchkes that were sold at the Cliffs of Moher gift shop!

Even my most Irish memories have gone up in smoke, so to speak. I remember hearing stories about my father's hardscrabble life growing up, in which he described cutting turf in the bog as a means to provide fuel and heat for the house. European and Irish governments have recently introduced laws that will prevent domestic turf cutters, who have been cutting turf for fuel for hundreds of years, from doing so. It seems ridiculous to have a natural resource lay idle and force the Irish to find costly fuel alternatives and downright criminal when one considers how it tears at our very Irishness!

I host an annual holiday open house for the family each New Year's Day, and I was struck by how many nationalities have infiltrated our Irish brood. My girls are half-Jewish and so is my godson and his sister. During December, we all hosted Christmas dinners and Chanukah menorah lighting get-togethers in the same week. My brother married an Italian/Polish woman. My cousin's twin boys are half Jamaican and do a credible Michael Jackson moonwalk.

I grew up in a Catholic enclave in Jersey City in which Irish, Italians, and Polish were the nationalities of choice. I didn't meet a Jewish person until we moved to the Central Jersey suburbs in seventh grade. Genetics and technology guarantee that my family's next generation will have a broader view of the world than I had growing up at the expense of some Irishness, and I don't think that's a bad thing.

Even though there were plenty of races and creeds huddled around the piano singing as my daughter played "When Irish Eyes are Smiling" on the piano during our open house, the chorus of voices was evidence enough that the tradition of tight Irish family ties was stronger than ever before.

The Jamaican Shamrock

Though I have been unlucky enough to have done a tour of every airport and train terminal in the United States, I am fortunate to have amassed enough frequent-flier miles from those trips to take my family on a nice vacation once every few years.

I will never forget the experience of disembarking from the plane and tumbling into that drab, secondary-market feel of Montego Bay Airport in Jamaica. My wife and I are insatiable reggae fans and the prospect of visiting the birthplace of Bob Marley was so strong that it overwhelmed any notion of common-sense parenting.

"I need to tell yah that it's a bit of a freaky place up there, mon," said the hotel concierge as she tried to make the arrangements for a tour bus to take us up the mountain. "A bit smoky up dem mountains, if yaknowwhatahmean." There was concern on her sweaty, blue-black face as she nodded in the direction of my daughters.

My wife bit her lower lip as I turned toward the kids.

"I need to explain something on how it works down here," I said before putting my index finger under the strap of my oldest's bikini top. "Y'know, there are places like Iran that would throw Annie here in jail for the bikini she's wearing now because the culture over there demands modesty in the female population. So, women cover up much more than here. Can you understand that?"

The girls nodded.

"Good. Well, here in Jamaica, marijuana is part of the culture. Where we're going, they use it in their religious worship. But back home where we live, marijuana is illegal and should never be brought to school. Can you understand that?" The girls nodded again.

"And you know that what we may see on that mountain is okay for the people of Jamaica but is not okay when we get home, right?" They were still tracking with me. I turned my gaze toward the concierge.

"Well, that settles it," I said with a smile. "Four tickets to Bob Marley's house tour, please!"

A black luxury tour bus rolled up into the open-air hotel lobby the following morning and we were greeted by a young girl with a rapid-fire mouth and a small knit beret in Jamaican colors. She was the tour guide, and a soft-spoken gentle giant of a man was the driver.

"Anyone know some Bob Marley tunes?" the girl asked. She led the crowd through most of *Legend*, Bob's popular greatest-hits package. "One Love." "Get Up, Stand Up." "Redemption Song."

She and I exchanged lyrics of lesser-known songs, egged on by the cheers of the other riders, and my daughters slid low in their seats, embarrassed by Dad's attempts to sing. The girl cackled in disbelief as I shouted the lines of "Kinky Reggae."

Uh, ah-oh-oh! I went downtown, (I went downtown)/ I saw Miss Brown; (said, I saw Miss Brown)/ She had brown sugar (had brown sugar) /All over her booga-wooga. (over her booga-wooga)/ I think I might join the fun, (I might join the fun)/ But I had to hit and run. (had to hit and run)/ See I just can't settle down (just can't settle down)/ In a kinky part of town.

"This motherfucker is crazy!" she squealed. "And he's the first one to get some smoke when we get up to Nine Mile!" My wife shot me a worried look.

Nine Mile is probably so named because it felt like we went nine miles uphill on our wide bus as the wheels hugged the treacherous tongue of a gravel ledge that clung to a mountain. Every bump that took the bus off balance felt like we'd tip over the edge of the mountain into the vegetation below. As we got closer, small stone wall structures painted in bright Caribbean colors jutted from the wild brush and the sun punished the tin roofs above them. The bus stopped at a general store and we were all treated to raw sugar canes. That kept the kids quiet until we reached our destination.

The village of Nine Mile is located in Saint Ann Parish. It is here, on Feb. 6, 1945, that the legendary king of reggae was born and it is in this very same place that he was laid to rest.

The natives were crowding the bus and banging on the windows as we drove through town. "Smoke! Smoke!" they chanted while a team of security guards formed a lane at either side of the bus. The gates of the Bob Marley Museum opened and we made our way into the compound.

My daughters' anxiety reached a boiling point as dreadlocked men approached the bus. I hadn't reached the last step before a man attempted to put a joint the size of the small end of a baseball bat into my mouth. I waved him away. I felt someone tug at the back of my shirt collar.

"That's garbage smoke, mon," said the bus driver. "He's the mon you want to see." I followed his long, fat index finger in the direction of a cinder block wall washed in salmon colored paint. There were two bricks missing in the wall and you could see a dark face peering from it. He put his finger through the wall and beckoned to us with his index finger. The bus emptied and a line formed at the wall. At the opposite side of the wall there was a wooden chalet with Bob's face near the triangular peak of the roof.

"Why don't you ladies run to the gift shop," I said. "I'll be along in a minute." My wife rolled her eyes, shook her head, and grabbed the girls' hands.

I had a choice to make there and then. Though the temptation of booze followed me everywhere I went throughout my life, I didn't have much experience with drugs. There was a flirtation with cocaine and Jolt Cola (three times the caffeine as regular cola!) during final exams during the college years, but I would like to think I was raised better than to get myself hooked on the seedier stuff. If my parents' good example wasn't enough, I had gone through college during the Reagan Administration's "Just Say No" drug era and had spent the better part of two decades in companies that routinely drug-tested their employees. There might have been a dabbling here and there when I was offered something, but I had never actually purchased illegal substances.

Was that the wind rushing in my ear or was that Haile Selassie I, the Ethiopian emperor worshipped by the Rastafari people, whispering words of wisdom? I could swear I could hear someone say, "Not smoking in this shithole would be like going to Hershey and not having chocolate, dumb-ass."

I took that as a divine sign and made my way over to the line by the wall. When it was my turn, the brown face lighted up to reveal yellowed teeth a shade lighter than the whites of his eyes. Every tooth was capped with scuffed gold.

"How much for some?"

"You'll like the exchange rate here," he replied, then broke out into an elongated laughter that I would hear from the mouths of nearly every worker on the compound.

"Give me $20 worth," I replied, handing him a crumpled bill. He disappeared for a second and then pushed a rolled joint as thick as two fingers and five inches long through the hole in the wall.

I tucked it in the bottom pocket of my cargo shorts and made my way toward the gift shop. The Bob Marley Museum and Mausoleum is located in Nine Mile and is managed by members of Marley's family. Strings of large flags in Jamaican colors with the words "Bob lives" licked the wind that blew above our heads while we took in the many historical artifacts: videos, guitars, awards, and photographs.

We walked through the museum and entered a small open-air theater, where an old man coaxed a reggae rhythm from the strings of a homemade instrument that looked like a banjo. Small children pushed branches through the space under the fence; the branches pierced hollowed-out juice boxes. "Spare change?" they'd ask, the sound of coins rattling like a tambourine while the man played.

We rested our heads on the Rasta-colored "rock pillow" on which Marley laid his head when seeking inspiration. I just got goose bumps writing that.

We made our way toward the white church at the top of the small hill. His body lies buried along with his guitar in an oblong marble mausoleum inside the tiny church of traditional Ethiopian design, the marble providing a cool reprieve from the baking sun outside.

We entered the cramped tin-roof shack that is Bob's birthplace. One can't help but be moved by the international movement of peace and music that was hatched by the humblest of beginnings; this must be akin to seeing the manger that held the infant Jesus in Bethlehem for a Christian.

We walked around the house to another shack with a simple sink and an orange clay oven. This was the spot where Cedella Booker, Bob Marley's mother, cooked the family meals. Today it was occupied by a small old man in a camouflage collared shirt and black beret. He was selling ganja tea, charging $5 for a small Styrofoam cup. While the girls bought bottled water, I sipped the tea.

After a simple fish and rice lunch, we made our way down the mountain. It was Good Friday and the bus stopped often as natives paraded through the town, their bare feet stomping in the dusty road as they carried large wooden crosses in their procession to imitate the death of Christ.

The girls were eager to cool off when we got back to the resort and they quickly changed into their bathing suits. I made my way to the balcony, remarking about how badly I wanted to finish writing this book. When the doors closed and I heard the elevator's ding, I made my way back into the room to spark up Daddy's souvenir! I don't remember much beyond that. After the first few puffs, the back of my head went numb and the least little thing became completely hilarious.

My days were spent hitting the spliff on the balcony, molesting the contents of the all-day buffet, giggling, grabbing an inner tube and paddling through the lazy river of water that rushed around the circumference of the resort like the baked cheerio that I was. Lather. Rinse. Repeat, mon!

I couldn't help but sing the lyrics to Peter Tosh's famous song while the pool water lapped at my flotation device.

Legalize it - don't criticize it

Legalize it and I will advertise it

It's good for the flu

It's good for asthma

Good for tuberculosis

...and it made for a great vacation!

OK, the last lyric was mine.

With one last, long inhale, I flushed the contents of my Costco-sized joint and my brief experience as a stoner down the drain. Responsible Dad kicked in and got all the passports in order. It was good while it lasted, mon!

Green Car in the Race to Nowhere

I just watched a riveting documentary called *Race to Nowhere*, which features the heartbreaking stories of young people across the country pushed to the brink in the hyped-up culture of achievement in our schools. Our public school sponsored a free viewing to ring the alarm bells with parents and educators who pack their kids' schedules with mountains of homework, activities, and worst of all, the expectation of perfection.

I never had to deal with that kind of pressure growing up. Sure, I entered kindergarten in the long shadow of my older cousins Debbie, Linda, Robert, and Diane. They were all conscientious, hardworking students who would rather rip up and rewrite a full page of perfectly handwritten work than turn in a page with a smudge or a folded corner. I was encouraged to be like them.

No, scratch that. My mom would sweat blood over her rosary beads praying for me to be a thoroughbred student but alas, her horse in the race was limping toward the glue factory academically.

I was a B and C student growing up, unable to concentrate on my lessons for very long and hopeless in organizing my uncomplicated life. "Needing poster board at 11 o'clock at night is now my problem?" screeched my mother as I panicked over the science project I forgot was due in the morning.

My little brother came up from behind, passing me by as he devoured the books and demonstrated the same perfectionist tendencies as our cousins. Add to the fact that he was a child prodigy on the drums and an outstanding soccer player, he was the one giving my mother plenty of bragging fodder. It took the emphasis off me and I suspect it left my parents praying for more, doubting I'd amount to much, but hoping for the best for me nonetheless.

Yet they never gave up on me. By some miracle that only a wad of "dead president flashcards" could produce, I found my way into a private school. St. Joseph's is an academic powerhouse nestled in the leafy suburb of Metuchen and I was sent there by the grace of hard work and sacrifice by my middle-class parents.

If I had given birth to a bulb as dim as I was, I never would have screwed him into a high-wattage school like that. I would have saved the money and bought a lifetime supply of fry-cook pants for my kid, but my folks were committed, at all costs, to fulfill on the immigrants' dream to have their kids turn out better than they did.

I suppose that constant undercurrent of pressure might be a distant cousin to the stress and urgency that kids in the *Race to Nowhere* film were suffering. There was also the expectation that you would rise above the kinds of jobs your parents were doing to put you through school and by God, you best not do anything that would embarrass our family name in the church parish. The thought of the wrath of God that would come down on my head when I did something that got the church ladies speaking ill of my family terrified me at the time. Now, I almost expect it to happen each week *The Irish Voice* publishes an edition or another novel is written.

There were other subtle pressures as well. "You're not living off me past 25 and if you find yourself in jail or spitting out a child before marriage, you can lose our number," my father would say.

I wonder today if my school track record would be different if I popped the potpourri of pharmacological candy that is available nowadays for every sliver of species on the attention-deficit spectrum. I know I had it back then and I have a touch of it as I write this—jumping from this essay to Facebook to playing with the Joker Pez dispenser on my desk to fumbling with my text messages to my iPod and then back to this column again!

My toes tapped incessantly when boredom set in during Sister Jane's first-grade class--was a shot of Restulex in order for that restless leg syndrome? My mind often wandered like a helium balloon—would it have been different if mom packed two Adderall in my Hot Wheels lunchbox?

I don't think it would have made a bit of difference. I was never a strong student; God gave me the gift of quick wit and creativity, skills they never taught in school but landed me this nifty title of vice president of sales and a view of the corner office near the top of this here corporate ladder.

In fact, the nuns tried to stamp humor and spontaneity out of their classroom with sensible low heels, and hands that moved their crayons outside the lines were quickly affronted with a ruler across the knuckles. We have evidence that these traits make great leaders like Steve Jobs and Richard Branson.

My girls make their way to the dining room table and crack open the books as soon as they get home from school, exerting more pressure on themselves than I ever would. My parents shake their heads in disbelief and frustration that I will not have the kind of kids who cause me the suffering my academic shenanigans did them. I pray this hard work will lead to streets paved with gold, but if the car turns onto a road to nowhere every now and then, I won't sweat it. Their dad turned out OK!

Remember Golden Deeds in Golden Years!

My wife and I have been perusing brochures of assisted-living facilities now that her mom has fallen harder and more often than the euro has this year. It reminds me of this recurring daydream that flash-forwards everyone into the future. My daughter, now 15, is 45 and she is pushing a large cart through the Costco warehouse. She is standing between a pallet of Depends Male Undergarments and the Kirkland store-brand adult diapers that *Consumer Reports* has just announced might run the risk of leaking on the sides. She labors over the decision in what to swaddle my incontinent fat white ass for a moment. Right before she chooses, the dream curtains part to reveal my 13-year-old daughter Maura, in her 43-year-old form, as she tours the wings of a nursing home. She stands between the brightly lighted ambient hotel vibe of the premium wing and the darker hallway that leads to rooms of boxy concrete blandness which emit a slight yet unmistakable smell of Frosted Flakes soaking in a bowl of stale urine. Maura nods politely as the manager weighs the pros and cons of their care plans.

When I am no longer competent to make choices for myself in that (hopefully) distant future and my children are at a fork in the road like the ones outlined in these dreams, I hope memories my daughters have of the stuff I have been doing for them all along inspires them to choose the name-brand adult diapers and the premium suite in the assisted-living facility instead of opting for the cheap route.

In case they forgot, here are just a few gentle reminders to the girls on things I did, which provide irrefutable proof that their dad deserves precious-metal treatment in his golden years.

Christmas morning: Yes, the present bounty that was laid at your feet was only possible from your dad's work and sharing his paycheck. That's a given. Yadda yadda yadda. The real work began after the presents were unwrapped. Those toys didn't just spring from their packages and run across the floor on their own! Tickle Me Elmo needed a battery enema up his furry red asshole before he started to giggle, and that required yours truly to drive to every 7-Eleven in a 30-mile radius for a few packs of Duracells on Christmas Day. With Elmo all sorted out, I turned to the Barbie that was crucified to her pink confines with wire twist ties to ensure she kept her position while in the shipping container sent from her Asian manufacturing origins. It was up to Dad to untwist her dozens of plastic-coated confines and at times I admit I wasn't successful at releasing her within an impatient toddler's timeframe. There could be more than one decapitated doll in the Central Jersey landfills that lost their heads when I lost my cool and forcibly yanked said doll from the package before her time. Rushing to Kmart on Christmas Day to replace Headless Barbie before you noticed the incident is yet another reason why only the best will do for Dad as you put him out to pasture!

Teenybopper concerts: Sure, it might look like I was enjoying myself immensely when I hollered the lyrics to Miley Cyrus' "The Climb," but I was just masking the pain of being subjected to a whole evening of bubblegum pop. Passing a kidney stone would have been a more joyous way to spend an evening. Yet I still would rather take in a Greyson Chance/Selena Gomez double bill than sit through Disney's Single Mom Princesses on Ice, Elmo Goes to the Proctologist on Ice, Bert and Ernie Come Out of the Closet on Ice, or Sesame Street's Intervention of Oscar the Grouch on Ice. Our basement is crammed with plastic wands, glow sticks, and hats that are reminders of those shows and evidence that I deserve the deluxe meal package at the nursing home.

Chuck E. Cheese: This most god-awful amusement and eating establishment on the planet was your favorite place on Earth for the first few years of your life. This was, of course, a germaphobe's nightmare; kissing a homeless man's balls would be cleaner than the yellow and red ones you joyously slobbered on while inside that giant meshed playroom. The silver Chuck E. game tokens have the words "no cash value" on them, something I confirmed the following day when I tried to use them as part of my co-pay when I had you in the pediatrician's office for a mysterious case of pink eye. Coincidence? I think not.

Dance recitals: Wading through three hours of interpretive dance, modern dance, ballet and company performances just to see you do that one tap number in the back line is torture at an incomprehensible level. Your mother sat next to me and she seemed to enjoy every minute of it while I plotted the murder of the dance school owner whose idea it was to sequence this many show tunes in rapid succession.

IKEA furniture: When you have kids of your own, I'm sure you'll mockingly tell stories of how your father would think he was following the Swedish instructions down to a "T" on your little art desk only to realize there were four screws left over and the drawer mechanism was facing the wrong way once everything was tightened up. You'd stand up in a fit of laughter, riffing on the way your dad would throw the widget tool across the room and scream, "F*cking live with it that way" before exiting the room with great dramatic flair.

Perhaps this might be a compelling reason to buy the store-branded adult diapers, come to think of it. Never mind. Are you listening, girls? Hopefully, I made my case!

High School Musical Love

I was starting to fall hard.

We had been in the car for over an hour and the banter couldn't be more free and easy between us. He laughed at my jokes and so did I. He had a dry and ironic sense of humor formed by one too many *Big Bang Theory* marathons and this suited me fine because that's my favorite show.

We started discussing music and squealed with delight over our common affinity for laid-back surfer rock. I guess the clincher for me was when he took out the ukulele and after fumbling for a few seconds, started to gently strum the instrument as he led a singalong of Jack Johnson tunes before ending his car concerto with "Let It Be" in a supple voice. Thank God I was driving. By gripping the wheel, I saved myself the embarrassment of losing my balance and falling into his arms outright. I had been waiting for years for a moment like this and my dream man was finally here!

I was falling head over heels for my future son-in-law!

My wife cautioned me. "You're jumping the gun, she's only 15. Plus, she says they're just friends. I don't think there's anything going on and I think you're heading for heartbreak, Daddy."

I was praying that she was wrong. Dads of daughters reading this know that the relationship you form with your little girl informs her view of any man that circles her orbit, including her mate. It's an enormous amount of pressure and possibility and you get no annual performance review or feedback of any sort to gauge your performance until Mr. Right or Mr. Wrong shows up on prom night.

I've invested 15 years in this kid by forming a relationship steeped in love, trust, and humor in the hopes that she wouldn't bring home some psycho loser. I viewed the news of a boy wanting to come over to study as a report card that graded my efforts. This young man in the rearview mirror was like looking at high honor roll!

That doesn't mean I have any intention of being a grandfather anytime soon and my eyes darted nervously between the road ahead and the rearview. It wasn't that long ago that I engaged in some backseat shenanigans with a girl in the dark while my date's parents drove us home from the movies. This boy was snuggling a little too close for comfort next to my daughter but it was only because the screen on his smartphone was small and he was trying to show her the video from his recent performance in a musical.

He then shifted in the seat and broke into spontaneous song from the show, which inspired my daughter to sing her favorite song from *Rent*, which triggered him to spin off one Broadway tune after another. As near as I could tell, he was keeping his "jazz hands" up above his head where I could see them while he sold the song to everyone in the car.

"Don't fall hard early," my wife warned. "She's going to play the field—and so should you."

Nonsense! This musical interlude brought on my daughter's delightful giggle and deepened my love for him as a son-in-law. Theirs would be a union that was factory buffed and vacuum sealed from any sexual or pharmacological impurities at a Walt Disney studio. The lights came on in the theater of my own mind. In tonight's performance of *High School Musical*, the role of Troy Bolton, originally played by Zac Efron, would now be played by my son-in-law; the part of Gabriella Montez originated by Vanessa Hudgens would be filled by my daughter! They would sing "Breaking Free" from the East High Auditorium set of the movie, a director would yell "cut," and my son-in-law would mambo down to the pub with me for a pint.

Instead, I had to settle for a handshake and a thank-you in the driveway from a polite young man raised so well that he offered to pay for his share of the gas before he closed the door.

"That is one great kid," I said, my voice trailing into a pillowy sigh.

"Whatever," said my daughter. "I couldn't get him to stop with the show tunes! I don't know how his girlfriend puts up with him."

I turned my head and choked an impending sniffle. My *High School Musical* dreams dashed, I throw the car in reverse. Alas, this was all much ado about nothing. Claudio from that Shakespearean play said it best:

"Let every eye negotiate for itself/And trust no agent; for beauty is a witch/Against whose charms faith melteth in blood."

Property Brothers for Sainthood

I just came back from vacation with the family in Los Angeles and I must say that a highlight of my trip was the Easter Mass I attended at St. Edward the Confessor Church in Orange County's Dana Point.

It was an expansive white structure with tight wings jutting from the church's center. The back wall was constructed entirely of glass, allowing worshipers to gaze across the majestic bluffs and onto the crashing waves of the Pacific Ocean below us. The rays of the sun were no match for the shiny, uplifting message of the sun-kissed priest, who used big screens and slide presentations to guide the worshippers through sermons and songs. I completely bought into this new multimedia expression of faith!

When I got home from vacation, there was an appeal from my parish waiting for me in the mail pile. They were pointing to the crumbling state of our church and asking parishioners for assistance to spruce up the House of God a bit. Left to their own devices, the stodgy old pastor and his blue-haired committee will probably use the cash to once again varnish over the cracked lacquered finish of the dark wood pews and reupholster the worn fabric on the kneelers.

Please! That look is so Spanish Inquisition! If only the Property Brothers were on our parish council. They are HGTV stud-siblings who help couples find, buy and transform extreme fixer-uppers into the ultimate dream home, using state-of-the-art CGI animation to uncover their vision of the future. They usually take only charity cases on the show, which is perfect for the Catholic Church because it has doled out so much money to sex-abuse victims that we now need a special collection to fix up the ol' place! I'm sure Jonathan and Drew would take pity on our poor parish and the Vatican as a whole.

Where would the Property Brothers begin? I'd say the first thing to go are these drab Stations of the Cross replicas that line the wall. I usually sit in the same pew each week, right next to the station that has Jesus falling for the third time. The poor guy looks like he's having a terrible time of it, agonizingly crumbling under the weight of the cross and looking up into his Heavenly Father as if to say, "Really, Dad? *Really*? You want me to drag this thing all the way up *what* hill? FML!

There are images of His swimmer's physique battered and laid on the wooden cross, like *Godspell* if the creators of True Blood imagined it. After a week of drudgery in the workplace, do you really need all these reminders of torture every place the eye lands on our day of rest? Maybe we can have HGTV's infectious David Bromstad, the pan-Asian host of *Color Splash*, paint some abstract cross-that-passes-as-tattoo art thingy that honors the suffering of Christ on the cross while simultaneously "bringing the room together"?

While we're at it, how about a little unfiltered sunshine instead of the gothic imagery of that stained glass? Natural light was invented when? 6th century? Listen, I love the intricacies of the art form as much as the next man, but some of the stained-glass artwork I've encountered is downright creepy. On one particular church from my childhood, there are images of sweet, milk-fed cherubs fluttering around the image of Jesus. They had adorable toddler faces, wings at the neck, and no body. As if the decapitation of children weren't chilling enough, the blue eyes and milky complexion would transform them into inky minions of Beelzebub when darkness hit the windows. I remember seeing an irritated bull with wings, an eagle with bloodless eyes, and a halo representing the gospel of saints Luke and John in some of the windows. Old McSatan had a farm, E-I-E-I-*no!*

Wouldn't some cozy pastel panes with depictions of sunrises, fish, and flower-encrusted crosses add a more soothing vibe to those badly needed conversations with our Maker?

You may think the whole premise is nonsense, but the church has done some remodeling of its own during the last 12 months. Back in November, the robes of Rome tweaked some of the words in our Liturgy and asked us all to embrace a new translation of the Mass that more faithfully tracks the original Latin. The Nicene Creed, the central profession of faith, now starts with "I believe in one God" instead of "We believe in one God." Communion now begins with the words, "Lord, I am not worthy that you should enter under my roof," instead of "Lord, I am not worthy to receive you." Church writers abandoned the modern (Vatican II) in favor of retro, like a canonical rewrite of *Mad Men*. I'm down with that, though my stomach gets upset when I think of how many millions they must have spent reprinting our missals instead of putting those bucks to work in the missions around the world.

Of course, the real house-cleaning that needs to happen in our church is as likely as finding a Pottery Barn catalog in the Jets locker room. We still have out-of-touch, white-haired pale men stifling modernity where it is needed most. Recent news was that the Vatican came down hard on the Leadership Conference of Women Religious for having the nerve to challenge outdated church teaching on homosexuality and the male-only priesthood, tarring and feathering the nuns for "radical feminist themes incompatible with the Catholic faith." The Vatican's purported intolerance in the area of pedophile priests seems hollow when you consider how since 2004 they've housed in its marble skirts the likes of Cardinal Bernard Law, the man who presided over decades of rampant abuse in New England.

The Property Brothers may be good at what they do, but the house is crumbling around us and they are not miracle workers. Still, is it too much to ask for a cushy accent pillow in that hard wooden pew for next Sunday's Mass?

Confession App

So, have you heard that the sacrament of Confession is going viral? According to an article in the *Los Angeles Times,* Little i Apps, LLC released Confession: A Roman Catholic App, which was developed under the supervision of Rev. Thomas G. Weinandy, OFM, executive director of the Secretariat for Doctrine and Pastoral Practices of the U.S. Conference of Catholic Bishops, and Rev. Daniel Scheidt, pastor of Queen of Peace Catholic Church in Mishawaka, Indiana.

I love the ingenuity here. Some creative minds came up with an innovative way to bring technology into a sacrament sorely in need of modernization.

I downloaded the app and went through the contents—genius! It is loaded up with prayers that include the Act of Contrition—no more fumbling through the lines!

One of the downsides—or upside, if the Lord is planning to take you soon—is the illuminating redraw of commandments into modern-life scenarios on the "examination of conscience" list on the app! According to this, committing adultery now includes using contraception in your marriage. This is for everyone's own good—do we really want more of me running around the planet? Number 8, bearing false witness against a neighbor, now includes gossip. Damn. Most of Ireland and their Irish-American brethren will be joining Perez Hilton on the Hades Latrine Cleaning Team if that's the case! Being married to the same woman for two decades, I thought I had Commandment No. 9, coveting thy neighbor's wife, handled. According to this list, you've sinned in this category if you've "allowed yourself to lose control of your imagination," "avoid banishing impure thoughts," or "read impure things online." Gulp! OMFG!

This brings me back to the time nearly 40 years ago when I made my first Confession. I was already weary of the dark wooden closets in the back of the church, the velvet curtain making the confessional look like upright coffins awaiting fresh bodies.

If that imagery wasn't enough to scare the bejesus out of a second-grader, Sister Henrietta was tasked with shepherding us through the process. She had a nervous tic and a manic personality that went from sweet grandmother to sadist in one ill breeze—think Joe Pesci in a veil if *Goodfellas* were filmed in a convent. She would pat you on the head if you got something right and give you an open-handed pimp-slap across your face if you flubbed a line.

"This examination of conscience scrubs your soul so that you're ready for God whenever he decides to call you home," she would say in her sweet voice just before the mania brushed across her face. Her jaw would stiffen as she continued. "And let me tell you, you don't want to be one of the little kids in hell. Kids your age haven't lived a long and wonderful life yet and that makes a child's time in hell more agonizing and wretched."

That set off a series of nightmares that had me taking a long dirt nap before I tasted the wafer later in the year. According to the Confession app, bearing false witness against the neighbor now includes being critical, negative, or uncharitable to others. Looks like this program was developed a bit too late for Sr. Henrietta, may she rest in peace!

Clean Up Yer Act

Thirty-eight miles separate my house from that of my mother's. Yes, I counted.

It takes about 50 minutes for Eileen's 77-year-old husband to drive her here, 63 if you count the pit stop at the pet store to get bully sticks for their grand-dogs to chew on. When my mother calls to announce that she is running errands in the area and would like to drop by for tea, we know we have an hour, give or take, to get the house in tiptop shape.

Being married to an Irishman has its benefits. We're usually the life of the party. We are proud, protective husbands and parents that go to extraordinary lengths to protect and love our family. But every rose has its thorn and an Irishman born of an Irish mother brings with it that mother's judgment of how you're keeping your house and looking after her son. My wife knows this drill and has gotten the pre-Eileen cleaning scene down to a science after 20 years of marriage.

In fact, we have a name for the whirl of mops and feather-dusting:

Eil-ifying. That means that floors must be swept, dishes are to be loaded into or out of the dishwasher, couches vacuumed, and piles of mail and magazines removed from the counter.

My wife even has a sense of humor about it at this stage. "Thank God for your mother in a weird way," she says as she scrubs the sink. "If it wasn't for her coming over once a week, who knows if anyone around here would lift a finger to clean this place!"

There are times when my wife isn't in the mood to run around the house with a mop, so she cagily suggests we meet my parents halfway at a diner for a meal instead. I thought that was one crafty way of avoiding an Irish mother's judgment on the quality of one's housekeeping skills, but after we had drinks with a few couples with whom we've become close, the stories I heard of how some women handle their Irish mothers-in-law made me laugh out loud.

"I hire a cleaning lady once a week and I time it as close to the weekend visit as possible," one said. "I have an episode of *Hoarders: Buried Alive* on the DVR and I pretend to be watching it as she comes over. She looks at the television at the very moment I say something like, 'Jeez, can you imagine anyone living like this?' It's a cheap shot, but it works."

"I couldn't be bothered," said another. "I sometimes spray Pledge around the house so it smells lemony and there is a hint that maybe I put some effort in. If she doesn't love me for who I am, that's her problem. Besides, she'll find something else to complain about, like how freezing it is in my house with all this air-conditioning. It's like she forgot what menopause is like or something." With that, she washed her resentment down with the rest of her margarita.

"Mine parks her broom on top of my house once or twice a year," one Polish woman said. "Right before she comes over, I go to the dollar store and pick up a selection of cheap get-well cards and I have the kids sign them. I put them on the mantel over the fireplace.

When she comes in and sees them and then the mess around her, she hugs me sympathetically and offers to clean my house without any judgment. She'll even throw a few soda breads in the oven on her way out to make sure we have enough to eat!"

Irish women of a certain age are sharp ladies, but this younger crowd seems up to their challenge. It takes about an hour to whip a house into shape and when that won't work, whipping up a line of malarkey will do just fine!

Pray for My Wife

There's a little magnet on the door of my refrigerator that says, "Pray for me, I married an Irishman." My Jewish wife bought it at a novelty shop while on vacation a few years back and it has become like a Buddhist's mantra that she has chanted, at times through a clenched jaw, ever since.

Take today, for example. We seem to have an ongoing disagreement on the definition of a house party. Her vision is a small and strategically picked exclusive guest list that will produce the perfect chemical reaction of spirited conversation over a succulent meal that allows her to try all those Food Network recipes she's been stockpiling with my girls.

My house party is more *Animal House* and if John Belushi and Martha Stewart had a baby, it would produce a host like me. The bigger the better, I always say and there is nowhere bigger than a Costco warehouse. When you can't turn the hat trick of turning loaves into fishes, this is the go-to place when you have to feed the masses. Dreams of frilly TV-show fare are mothballed in favor of feeding the masses with pillow-sized bags of chips, sleeves of frozen burgers, and tubs of brownie bites that will play well with a belly full of Guinness at the end of the night. As a precaution, I make the last-minute decision to stock up on black trashcan liners for the base of the toilet in case someone blows groceries in our small half-bath. Might as well pick up a fistful of fresh flowers near the checkout too, to place as a peace offering on the altar of a woman who has been chanting "Pray for me, I married an Irishman" since we woke up this morning.

The flowers were a good call. The fact that I'm upstairs typing this little missive while the house sits in disrepair a mere three hours before 36 people descend on our backyard has created muck-thick tension in our home.

"Lighten up," I say patronizingly. "The grillmeister general has everything under control, m'love."

She ain't buyin' it. Any woman reading this knows what happens next. The "I cook/you clean" bargain struck between man and wife on the morning of the barbecue means that I marinate my liver in booze while I flip the marinated chicken on the barbie a few times for a grand total of twenty minutes. While I am doing this, she will spend the rest of the night arranging the side dishes, serving snacks, fetching drinks, ushering our drunk friends around the house with coasters and Windex, loading the dishwasher, unloading the dishwasher, ensuring everything is put back in its place, and when it's over, she lovingly guides me upstairs into the guest bed because the snoring and belching required to shake off a hangover of this magnitude will prove too much to sleep through.

"These beers are room temperature," my wife says, passing the office as I type this. "You better get a move-on and get some ice."

I'll sign off for now in search of something as cold as the tone in her voice. But first, I'll stop at a church and say a decade of the rosary for my loving and patient wife, who did nothing to deserve being married to this particular Irishman. It's gonna be a long summer and she's going to need all the prayers she can get.

Screw U Haiku

When you get that first book published, your writer friends think it was just a fluke.

After the second one drops, they think, *this guy might know what he's doing* and they come to you with their half-baked manuscripts and book ideas. You offer to help and before long, you're in deep therapy trying to unlock why they keep stopping themselves from pursuing this dream.

Two friends came to me with some literary promise: Jennifer assembled 100 beautiful poems after crawling out of the pit of doubt dug by a callous professor in her recent past. Charlie, a small, biting, bitter soul whom I've loved since college, wrote a misshapen list of things that pissed him off called *Gripes*.

I toggled between the two works for weeks on my desktop until a collision of chocolate and peanut butter in my head led to some sweet Reese's inspiration!

The Irish Republican Army taught the world a thing or two about rage and our homeland is rife with brilliant poets like Brendan Behan and Samuel Beckett. A collection of poems—about gripes and the things that anger me. Why didn't I think of this sooner?

I became fascinated with the limits of the haiku in storytelling and from those confines sprouted creativity. Well, I'll let you be the judge of that.

It's not Yeats, but of course, you had low literary expectations when you bought this book and why didn't you buy his shit instead if that's what you wanted? Make up your mind!

Picked last in gym class

Humiliating? Ya think?

Tears on my man boobs.

Writer man hot now

Didn't think so at prom time

You're in next novel.

My beach has these clumps

Of fake-tan New York white trash.

Seagulls, shit there please!

White suburban teen

Blasting rap from car speakers

Poops pants in real 'hood

Dad, we need a pet

Promise to care for our pug

Dog shit on rug stays.

Work crews jamming roads

Only work of day

Making coffee into piss

Hey, plane-seat makers!

Seats shrink, asses get wider

Take aisle seat in hell!

Writing not that hard

Look listen scribble edit

Rinse, lather, repeat.

Facebook profile pic

Of ex thirty years ago

Thirty pounds ago

Liver black as night

Drink shots and pints til daylight

White Castle in sight!

Kid outta college

So full of promise and hope

Life will break you soon!

Comic book reader

Well into your forties now

Man-child still single

Your cell phone ring tone

Cartoonish and immature

Kills you in board room

"When I was your age,

We worked hard for allowance."

Wow. Sounding like Dad!

First time I had sex

It was dark and so scary

I was by myself

Ryan Seacrest smiles

A cold grin that has no soul

Your makeup is flaking...

Sports fans annoy me

Shout at TV, follow scores

I could give two shites!

Robbery at 20,000 Feet

I took the family on a vacation about a month ago, so now the credit card bills are coming in. I'm looking here at two line items, each for $32, which have been billed as in-flight food and entertainment from United Airlines.

You see, a trip from California to Newark would have been unbearable, cruel, and inhumane without the use of the in-flight Dish Network entertainment system that is embedded in the back of the seat in front of us. With a swipe of the credit card, you are $8 lighter but you have six hours of movies and cable television to keep your mind off those cramped conditions in coach. It would also be cruel and inhumane not to feed the family, so another $8 per head and we each have a "sweet n' savory box" of goodies. I would have ordered a Guinness to wash it all down, but the card had been maxed out.

When I was my daughters' ages—*Wow! Sounded just like Dad there for a minute!*—I took the flight every other year from JFK to Shannon Airport. The duration of the flight was roughly the same as the Los Angeles cross-country travel we do now, depending on the prevailing headwinds.

Of course, that doesn't include the time actually getting to the airport on the Belt Parkway. It was only about 50 miles from Jersey City, but the unpredictable Belt could mercilessly add an unplanned hour to that trip. If you had to get to the Aer Lingus counter two hours before your flight, the crow's flight was an hour, the clogged Beltway allotment would tack on an hour, and my father's compulsive ways would require you to be an hour early wherever you went, so we would leave at 3:30 for a 9 PM flight.

"Look at those green mountains, Dad!" I would exclaim from the back of the car as we slunk past the Fresh Kills on Route 440 through Staten Island. "They look like the Galtee Mountains near Granny's house!"

The driver, his thumbs drumming on the steering wheel to let off nervous steam, would roll his eyes and turn to my mother.

"This eejit thinks the landfill piles are the mountains. Is there any hope for him?"

More often than not, the Belt Parkway would behave and the journey that was supposed to take three hours took about 60 minutes. That meant that we would be at the airport with tickets in hand and bags checked at 4:30 for the 9 PM flight.

"Now, g'wan, better to be early than to be sorry," my dad would say amidst our protests that we could have swum to Ireland faster than this journey he had planned. "Ye'd be whinin' about the vacation bein' ruined if we were still stuck on that godforsaken road." With that, he would fish through his pockets for loose change and my brother and I would split a few packs of Life-Savers or M&Ms for those three hours in the waiting area.

Of course, you wouldn't pay for a thing once you boarded the plane and there were no television monitors to keep you entertained. Who could see the screen with all that cigarette smoke billowing above you, and what did it matter that you were in the nonsmoking section? Weren't we all in the same cramped tube breathing in the same air? We would land at Shannon, our lungs charred with the smoke and completely knackered by the jetlag and what amounted to a 12-hour journey when you factored in the wait time.

The only thing we'd have to show for the trip would be the Aer Lingus teaspoons that we'd all be instructed to pack in our bags before the stewardesses (yes, that's what we called them back then) removed our service trays. When I questioned the motives behind this theft, I was told the spoon dispensed the perfect amount of sugar for "the tay."

Looking at the screwing I got from United on my credit card bill, I am thinking about those sweet times we'd screw over the airlines for a sugar spoon. Those were the days.

Don't Mess with the Nuns

Much ink has been devoted in *The Irish Voice* about the Catholic Church lately, with some of our columnists locked in an epic battle with the readers they serve. There seems to be a chasm of debate as to whether our church has gone off the deep end, with my esteemed colleagues tendering as evidence Catholic hospitals coughing up a hairball over the President's mandate of reproductive health coverage, and Catholic universities barring commencement speakers who espouse views inconsistent with church teaching. Now comes irrefutable proof that the Vatican has lost touch with reality altogether.

They're messing with nuns.

It was recently announced that the Vatican has decided to rein these powerful women into the fold, ordering American nuns to hand control of their group over to a trio of bishops because they fear the nuns have lost Rome's conservative narrative. The Leadership Conference of Women Religious, whose members represent about 80% of nuns in the United States, issued a sharp statement calling the Vatican's rebuke unsubstantiated and "the result of a flawed process that lacked transparency." The nuns say the Vatican's report has "caused scandal and pain throughout the church community and created greater polarization," according to widely published statements.

It makes you wonder if nuns educated our current pope and the cardinals; if that were so, they would never think about crossing those women—certainly not the ones I encountered in my business career.

I was educated by these gals in Jersey City, a fact I immortalized on a T-shirt that says "you can't scare me—I was educated by nuns." I'm sure my boyhood imagination amped up the nightmare factor, but I swear the only time I saw any one of them smile or act joyful was when their founder, Mother Elizabeth Ann Seton, was canonized by the pope in 1975, when I was in the fourth grade.

I thought I would leave the Irish nuns behind me when I left school and entered the working world, but that was not the case. I landed a job selling laboratory supplies to hospitals in the Pennsylvania Dutch region and I found these veiled ladies at every level of one institution. I remember having to negotiate pricing on test tubes and petri dishes with Irishwoman Sister Jane. My company could never get far with Sister Jane until I had overheard from someone how her morning routine included attending Mass in the hospital chapel before hitting the storeroom to check inventory. Mass started at 6:30 AM and I lived an hour away, but I was in that chapel each Tuesday: stockroom order day. Despite being a grown man in a power suit, I would allow a wide berth between the diminutive, stooped woman and myself. She would shuffle through the aisles, squinting constantly as I followed behind her with an order pad. Her negotiations were brutal and she employed the most powerful weapon in an Irishwoman's arsenal: guilt.

"Sharpen your pencils, young man," she would croak. "I know everyone has to make a living but every dollar of profit you take for yourself is a dollar I can't spend on the poor in this community."

I grew my business exponentially as I won the old gal over and I was grateful for the lessons from her keen business sense. I needed those lessons when I eventually moved up the ranks and into the Big Apple to face Sister Kate, a hospital administrator in lower Manhattan. In this business setting, she wore a sensible navy suit and flat shoes with no veil. Sister Kate had a keen mastery of healthcare trends, balancing her enormous hospital's expenditures against the harsh New York reimbursement climate. The hospital was buckling under the demands of charity care in Manhattan, a situation made worse by the HIV pandemic gripping the city at the time. Although she had ditched the veil long ago, her head was still weighed down with the concern of the poorest of the poor in the surrounding neighborhood.

Of course, she would never show me that passionate side. She had a major ax to grind with pharmaceutical and diagnostic companies that boasted about these huge profits in the earnings statements she seemed to have memorized. Perhaps it was a negotiation ploy, but she ignored the line item about the amount of cash we generated for research and development to continue the high standard of care she expected.

"Just adding bells and whistles that no one needs, young man," she scoffed. That's what dealing with her was like. I applied my charm and humor on this steely woman but she seemed immune to it. That all changed the day we came from the cafeteria (where she bought her own stuff so it didn't look fishy that I was buying her favor with a $3 tuna sandwich) and I said, "That's something you don't see every day," when I passed an image of a nun in stained glass.

"You know who that is?" she asked incredulously.

"Yes, Sister," I replied nervously. "That's Elizabeth Ann Seton. She was the first U.S. citizen to be canonized and was the founder of the order of the Sisters of Charity nuns that educated me in Jersey City."

Her stone face cracked a smile, slowly at first, then she beamed brighter than the light in the stained glass.

"You might be one of the good ones after all," she said. "She founded my order and those ladies in St. Ann's are my sisters. Now I know why I like working with you so much!"

I'm praying those three unfortunate Vatican bishops catch a lucky break like that during their first visit with the Leadership Conference of Women Religious....it's gonna be a tough room indeed!

A "Tail" of Woe

You just know your day isn't going to get off to a great start when you are awoken by your spouse shouting, "Ohmygodgetdownhererightnowohmygod!"

You run past the full coffeepot that contains the elixir so desperately needed to face the world so that you can address the unfolding emergency in the backyard. Your Chihuahuas, those pint-size dogs with the courage and attitude of Rottweilers, have their yipping little barks drowned out by the most bloodcurdling screeches imaginable. You try rubbing the sleep from your eyes, squinting hard to see what has their attention at the fence.

Sophie, the brown dog, boldly approaches the edge of your property and brazenly bites into the bushy tail wedged in between two tight slats of your wooden fence. She flails her head from side to side violently, her eyes overcome with bloodlust, determined to remove the tail from the skeleton of whatever the hell is on the other side of the fence. This begins a more vigorous stream of chattering and screeching from the animal, which is understandably upset and annoyed that another four-legged creature is chewing on the base of its spine.

Our hero hastily hopscotches over the piles of dog excrement that his daughters swore up and down they were going to pick up this weekend, and closes in on the action. The pups are shooed away and then snatched up and unceremoniously dumped into the house.

I'm now left alone, not only with the back end of a battered and bloodied wounded animal of unknown species, but with my own inadequacies as well. My Athenry-born father married a gal from Limerick, both good farming stock who combined have probably killed more chickens and pigs for their own survival than there are dogs in my town. Heck, they have also slaughtered enough predatory foxes in the family henhouses to make coats for Lakers! Here I am, the flaming Yank Narrowback, so far removed from that murderous lineage that I find myself getting lightheaded with each step toward the tail.

In all likelihood, the dogs chased this thing through the fence and the tail got snagged. As the dogs tussled with it, the animal pulled harder, hopelessly wedging it farther up the slats in the fence. I looked over the fence, first to see what species I was dealing with, and then to catch the eye of the state trooper next door who might be heading out the door on his way to work.

I'm so disgusted with myself—desperately seeking a real man to help this damsel-esque character with his shamrock pajama bottoms and matching T-shirt. No, it was time to pull on the big-boy pants and take care of this like a man! I dashed into the shed, unhooked the handle of the spade from the nail that it hung on, and approached the tail one more time. Like lancing a boil, I charged at it, bringing my weight down on the tail and freeing it from its wooden wedge.

The animal, dazed from the shock of it all, slowly slithered under the fence and clawed toward freedom in the neighbors' yard. I still don't know what manner of creature it was and I'm not sure if it survived, but I was clear that it wasn't my problem any longer.

My bravery took my wife and daughters by surprise

"You took care of it yourself?"

"You didn't have to call Pop-Pop (*Editor's note: that's my dad*) down for this? Really?"

News of the adventure made it to the fence of the state trooper, an avid hunter, who took to calling me "Squirrel Killah" every time he has met me on the lawn ever since. They can mess with me all they want, but I know I went all alpha-male and grabbed the situation by the tail when I needed to. Sorry, couldn't resist.

Book 3: Cultural Commentary

I have filed a column in **The Irish Voice** *each week for more than a decade. In* **This Is Your Brain on Shamrocks,** *I included some columns on my favorite albums of the last decade that some readers loved because it gave them some leads to new music. If you're one of those readers, this is for you.*

If you're not one of those readers, well, this section is pretty short. Skip to Book 4!

Parting Is Such Sweet Sorrow...Reflections on The Pogues' Farewell Tour

The claustrophobia of a sweaty, packed club. Hopscotching over vomit and spilled beer. The excruciatingly long lines to both purchase and eliminate beer. I'm sure the combination of all those things made me look to the heavens and sigh, "I'm too old for this sh*t" as I bowed out early on the Pogues show, "A Parting Glass," at Terminal 5 on St. Patrick's Day.

At first I panicked when I read into the "parting glass" reference as a hint of retirement; the band reformed at the turn of the century and we've all become so accustomed to an annual visit from the lads each March that the possibility of the world without touring Pogues was one we wanted no part of.

"It does and it doesn't mean retirement," guitarist Phil Chevron said in an interview with me. "It is *A* Parting Glass, not *The* Parting Glass. We have been doing it longer than this lineup existed—1987 to 2003. We have been in this lineup since 2001 and this is a moment of pause to see what to do next. It marks the end of a phase. There is a keenness to do some new things as well. We are artificially putting a stop to this phase of our career. It has been a nice surprise for us but it might be time for something else."

I am not filing a bad review here. The Pogues are legends for good reason; very few bands are capable of streaming sparks from banjoes, flutes, and accordions the way The Pogues can. Every nicked note and nuance of Flogging Molly and Dropkick Murphys can be heard in the band's "Streams of Whiskey," a cultural tour de force that spun the crowd into a dizzying whirlpool of cheers, fist pumps, and sing-alongs. "If I Should Fall From Grace with God" brought a similar reaction. At that point I looked around to see slack jaws on fans not born when *Rum, Sodomy & the Lash* came out. It somehow validates your own slavish devotion to the band and in a more smug moment, you snicker, "You won't find JLo judging this on *American Idol,* kiddies!"

Indeed, you wonder what Randy Jackson, Lopez, and Steven Tyler would make of a singer like Shane MacGowan if he was just starting out now. At 53, he shuffled onstage in a way that hinted at an inability to twist his waist; it was as though one of his lower vertebra was fused to his hip. He was dressed entirely in black, including the knit cap and dark glasses. The spotlight shone on everyone brightly this evening, yet his illumination was a dark-blue hue, creating a 'Paddy the Cryptkeeper' vibe that was simultaneously creepy and captivating. He might be a broken shell of his former self, yet he has more charisma in his yellowed and tarred forefinger than the new crop of *Idol* hopefuls combined.

I can report that the singer was swilling liquid all night, but it looked from my vantage point like Poland Spring instead of poitín, though toxicology reports were inconclusive as of this writing.

His voice is less of a voice nowadays; the grunts and slurs make his contribution more like an instrument that joins the flutes and fiddles. We've grown accustomed on these reunion shows to that beautiful Pogue prose spit out of a rotted mouth that coughs up cemetery dirt, but when he sat in a chair and sang "Waltzing Matilda," the audience heard a voice that was clear and spine-tingling.

It was odd and highly amusing to overhear a conversation debating how the lead singer's new teeth will impact his singing. Tonight, those new choppers in his gob are akin to restringing a lute in an orchestra.

While it was a satisfying evening of the old standards delivered by the best in the business, there was a part of me that felt a little awkward and foolish about the whole evening. It was like spending time with a college buddy 20 years after graduation, finding little in common while trying to avoid the topic that everyone in the room is middle-aged.

I'm forty-something with kids and a mortgage in the suburbs, and I am no longer a Hot Topic punk rocker. Some of the Pogues are old enough to be grandfathers, no longer new and dangerous themselves. Maybe Phil Chevron is right: it might be time to swallow the contents in this parting glass and raise a toast for something new between us when and if we ever meet again.

My Big Fat Gypsy Wedding Review

I'm not much of a reality TV watcher, but the constant onslaught of teasers and trailers for *My Big Fat Gypsy Wedding* tempted me like the smell of baked nom-noms wafting out of an Auntie Anne's pretzel kiosk. For years I was fascinated by the traveling caravan communities perched alongside Irish roadways. The gypsies selling oils and scarves on the cobblestone walkways were an exotic delicacy in the sea of pale people and thanks to the good folks at The Learning Channel, I got a virtual all-access pass into the mysterious shadow of Irish culture of nomads known as the traveller people

Mind you, *travellers* was not the first name I heard to describe these people—*tinkers* and *knackers* was more like it, with these nouns usually prefaced by the pejorative word *feckin'*. One mild-mannered uncle on my dad's side grips the steering wheel hard and spits curse words every time he passes the new government housing in the section of Tuam where the travellers live. "Faith'n they're a fair bit nicer than the house I broke my back to build," he'd shout in disgust. I have seen firsthand the mounds of trash they left on our family's fields when someone pressed them to move on and though there was never proof, I have heard friends and family blame them for every petty crime in the bog.

Of course, these bile-tinged accusations only added to my curiosity when I tuned into the first episode of *Wedding*. Like all television in this programming genre, the camera casts a wide eye on white trash, playing into their stereotypes for the pleasure of the film crew. An 8-year-old girl emerges on her Communion day from Mama's trailer with false eyelashes, a spray tan, faux rhinestones along her eyelids, and a taffeta dress so large it has trouble fitting between two parked cars. She joins her little prosti-tot friends at the party afterward and no girl on the dance floor is over 10, and no heels are less than 6 inches. Despite assurances of purity, morality, and spirituality from a self-professed traveller expert on the program, the puddles of flesh spilling out of the tight gowns on the big wedding days looked more like a brothel on prom night than a bridal party. Perceived slights from the macho young men in the trailer park are settled—where else?—behind the cement wall at the back of the trailer park in a bare-knuckle brawl that the announcer assures us is a traveller ritual.

The breakout stars of the show are Paddy and Roseanne Doherty, the owners of one trailer park. "Queen Elizabeth has her place but I swear to God and my babies, this is my Buckingham Palace," Paddy announces before hopping into his convertible Audi (he gets a new car every six months whether he needs it or not). A former bare-knuckle boxing champion, Paddy, 52, has painted "PD" on the blacktop in front of his trailer park, a fitting coat of arms for the likes of him if ever there was one. He is a study in conflicts, a man who cries at his son's grave while delivering rough justice to anyone exhibiting domestically violent behavior within the comfort of their trailer if it happens to be parked on his land. With his bulging biceps and affinity for sleeveless shirts, he looks like a cross between a juicing Fred Flintstone and The Situation's Neanderthal ancestor.

"You'd never see a traveling man shopping," he says without a hint of irony as he lies on a store mattress. The camera pans across the store and finds his wife looking at a white-lacquered dining room set that's so gaudy it would give Elvis Presley vertigo. His purpose is soon clear when it comes time to pay the bill and Paddy takes yer man out back to hammer out a price. "Even if you give a traveling man a pound off the price, he feels like he got a good deal," muses Roseanne. With her cottony bleached hair, rhinestone jewels in the shape of a crown on each back pocket, and loopy mannerisms, she could easily be the main character in every Loretta Lynn or Judd song.

One recently married bride explains that education is not something that's much regarded in the traveller community.

Really? Ya don't say! I kinda figured that out when I saw Irishman Johnny leave his trailer home, hop in a helicopter, ride to his reception, and take the ring out of a pouch held in the talons of a trained owl that flies to him. If he had any education in math, he'd know that money spent on this costly circus could be put to better use....*Oh, I dunno. How about a new set of teeth for the missus?*

When Paddy and Roseanne pull up to their son's grave and she begins to sob uncontrollably while a crowd of travellers drink beer around the grave, your heart goes out to her. I soon joined her in a cry with the knowledge that I'd never get the three hours back that I wasted watching this marathon of *My Big Fat Gypsy Wedding*—nor will I ever recoup the time spent watching the rest of the episodes.

What Your Irish Music Says About You

I recently saw a friend with whom I hadn't connected in many moons. "You *still* writing for the *Irish Voice*?" he exclaimed. "Boy, have you done a great job milking that diddly-diddly beat 'til it's dry!"

Yes, I hang out with the most charming people.

"This just shows how little you know about my peeps," I said defensively. "What's cool about the Irish and Irish-American music community is that we've produced a wide spectrum of sounds and styles while still sticking to the Celtic voodoo that we do so well. We make a flavor of music for any palate!"

And don't Irish music fans come in all flavors? You can tell a lot about a person by what you see in his or her record collection or taste in concerts. I've been going to Irish concerts for 15 years or more in this job and I've stared down many a crowd. What's more, I *am* Irish, which means I have a dominant judgmental gene that entirely qualifies me for a snarky opinion on everyone I see at these concerts. Submitted for your consideration is a list of music choices and what they might say about you:

Celtic Woman: Without fail, you take the mothballs off that QVC Arran sweater you got during the last Paddy's Day home shopping marathon. You fidget with the rabbit ears atop the television until

PBS is crystalline, and your breath is taken away at the sight of those lasses in all their sparkly taffeta glory. Coming to this show for some Irish culture is like cooking a meal in the Barbie kitchen, yet there you are, ready to plunk down your donation at pledge time for that latest disc of saccharine-coated culture. When it's time to get off the La-Z-Boy recliner to actually see the live show at Radio City, your hair is dyed a burnt cheddar just for the occasion, your Tara brooch has pinned the Book of Kells silk scarf around your neck (in case it's drafty), and you are ready to rock!

Van Morrison: You've been listening to this guy for years; heck, he's been your wingman on any lucky flight in love that you've taken. A little *Astral Weeks* here, a dash of that rakish brogue there, and soon your bedfellows were waking up without knowing or caring where their undergarments went. But now, Van is older and so are you. That hippie vibe is intoxicating, which probably explains why you felt the need to take that thick wallet from the back pocket of your expandable- waist Dockers and plunked down the gold Amex to purchase a block of $250 tickets to that last Astral Weeks Memory Lane Tour that Van did a few years back. You used to screw to Van, but now Van is screwing you. And you kinda like it.

Celtic Punk Rock: You are almost certainly male and mad at the world in general, and especially sore at the Hot Topic store manager in particular. He's the guy who tried to schedule you on the cash register the night your favorite band is in town. The nerve of him! Your bands play loud 'n' proud 'n' bold and this is the soundtrack of your seething discontent with the bad hand that life has dealt you. Leather jacket? Check. Jackboots? Check. Little metal chain that connects your belt loop to the wallet with no money in it? Check, check, check! With all those fists pumping in the air and those lyrics shouted with such force that you pop a vein, this is the place you've chosen to expel life's bad stuff faster than a colon full of White Castle hamburgers. The closer you come to the mosh pit, the more likely it is that you have been accused at some point of assault and battery. But what harm? You've never been convicted of the two at the same time. Plus, didn't the chick have it coming?

Sinead O'Connor: You're either a leather-clad, high priestess badass that's snarling at the world or married to someone who is. There is no in between.

The Wolfe Tones, Derek Warfield and the New Wolfetones, or any other rebel trio banjo band with "Wolfe" in its name: You're one of the many who didn't get the office memo circulating around, which announced that "the Troubles" ended decades ago. Just when you began to let go of all that anger directed at the Brits, along came Simon Cowell to prove once again that those limey bastards are the devil incarnate. You've brought along your son or nephew to this show to teach him about his heritage, but it's no use. He orders a Guinness and Harp mixed pint when the band plays "Come Out Ye Black and Tans" without a hint of irony. He thinks an Irish car bomb is a Guinness with a shot in it and Bobby Sands was some extra in *The Hunger Games*. He's not paying a bit of attention to the lyrics but in the end, you find one thing that you can agree on: a fist-pumping rebel song does the trick when you're punishing your liver!

Daniel O'Donnell: You are a close cousin to the Celtic Woman fan; heck, you may even have some of their CDs mixed in with "The Daniel." The thing that sets you apart from the other species is that you bring all of the disappointments of parenthood to these shows. *This* boy never makes his mother wrong or blames him for how screwed up he is, not like that no-good son that came from your loins. See how he blows a kiss to his mammy from the balcony—it would take an act of God to get your *amadaun* to say "I love you" at the end of his obligatory Sunday afternoon phone call. And let's not get you started on that daughter-in-law! On the rare occasion that she grants you access to your grandchildren, you have attempted to expose them to the wholesomeness of The Daniel instead of that tramp Rihanna. They plug their earbuds in and tune him out, much to your chagrin.

Your sons and daughters have met behind your back to see what to do about your dementia. They are pointing to the fact that you've organized a bus trip to go see Daniel in Branson, to include a stop at every religious shrine to the Blessed Mother along the way, as proof that you've lost your marbles.

Loreena McKennitt, Enya, and the like: You are almost certainly a woman, have more than one pair of yoga pants, and get indignant when someone refers to God as a male. Let your high school friends from Crestwood walk around with their Michael Kors handbags; your tie-dyed knapsack with the peace signs holds a wallet just fine, thank you very much! Cubicles are for chumps—you can make money in any room that has oil and a massage table. You have a perennially active profile on Match.com because you are sick and tired of dating Dungeons & Dragons masters, but the real secret behind your lack of dates has everything to do with those Birkenstocks.

Reading Into My Influences

I always feel that my selections of writers that have inspired me are too lowbrow to belong to an Irish-American writer, like asking a sommelier about the merits of box wine.

I should have some advanced, pretentious literary tastes. I should join my fellow Irish writers in the many Bloomsday celebrations around Manhattan, an invite I've repeatedly declined because I can't make heads nor tails of James Joyce. For me to read *Ulysses* would be akin to watching *Real Housewives of Atlanta* while poking my eye with a toothpick. No thanks.

Is it wrong of me to say I enjoy the kinds of stories you'll find mass-marketed in the Hudson News kiosks at the airport? A good novel by Stephen King or John Grisham has just as much ability to entertain as *Catcher in the Rye*. Plus, J.D. Salinger couldn't pump out the consistent quality that those authors can, so that should count for something.

So, here is the list of my fellow Irish writing compadres that have moved, touched, and inspired me over the years. Judge not lest you be judged.

Dennis J. "Denny" O'Neil, DC Comics in general and Batman in particular: Scoff all you want about naming a comic book writer and editor as an influence. Why don't you try telling a story with just a few dialogue bubbles hanging over the mouths of your drawn subjects? You can't really waste a word inside those bubbles and you have to keep the story line moving along so that pictures and words flow together. Isn't that what a good writer does? His stories, when combined with the artwork of Neal Adams, were a huge influence on me when I set out to tell stories myself. I did attempt to draw comics throughout my high school years and they were abysmal compared with the high art of O'Neil and Adams.

Mary Higgins Clark, *Where Are the Children?* She was not the world's bestselling suspense writer when my teacher put this on my summer reading list in 1975. This was her first published book, a tale that set off a summer's worth of nightmares. I recently went back to the story and was shocked that there was no bloodshed or a harsh word in the telling of this tale; the same cannot be said for the pulpy horror books that would consume most summers. I have read many of Ms. Clark's books since then and they have always kept my interest. I particularly loved *On the Street Where You Live* (Simon & Schuster, 2001), set in my hometown of Spring Lake Heights, and her autobiography *Kitchen Privileges*, which was published the same year. I have had the pleasure of interviewing her many times over the years. A conversation with her, over tea on her front porch that year, about the writing process was one that kicked me in the ass to start writing myself. I'll go to my grave remembering that chat with one of the greats.

Frank McCourt, *Angela's Ashes:* This is the book that made me want to be a writer. I was first drawn to the cheap use of words and the run-on sentences that he used to describe his boyhood world through the eyes of a child. You laugh at the humor he lays out to describe his father and friends drinking the paycheck away in the pubs, and your throat gets lumpy as the consequences of doing that amidst the abject poverty sets in. McCourt's name is a hotly contested one at my family's dinner table; my mother forbids the mention of his name in our house. She is from Limerick as well, is about the same age, and feels qualified to judge the book as a pack of lies that shamefully paints his hardworking mother in a negative light.

I'm not sure if this is a pack of lies, but I do know my life was never the same once I put down that book. I am so grateful to have had the opportunity to tell him that in the snug of a pub shortly before he died.

Roddy Doyle's Barrytown Trilogy: *The Snapper, The Van, and The Commitments:* I remember participating in an up-and-coming Irish writer's salon back in 2005, shortly after my first novel was released. There were nine of us on the bill and we were all asked to read from our favorite authors. Without talking with one another, seven of us picked passages from Doyle's books. What does that tell you?

No one touches Doyle when it comes to spinning a tale with little more than a few lines of dialogue. The stories in this trilogy are light on details of what the room looks like and what someone was wearing. It is propelled almost entirely by dialogue that is so authentically steeped in the rhythm of a Dubliner's unique cadence that it leaves me striving to become a better dialogue writer every time I read one of his books.

All of these books were made into movies based on their spot-on take of modern Ireland. *The Commitments'* soundtrack spawned the best soul album ever made on Irish soil. That alone should put Roddy on this list!

Brendan O'Carroll, *The Mammy, The Granny, and The Chiselers:* Another winning trilogy that was a huge influence. Irish humor with heart is the vibe that runs through these three books, centered on Agnes Browne and her family. From the first few pages, when Agnes is burying her husband, follows the wrong hearse into the graveyard, and brawls with the other widow, the laughs do not stop. I love the scene where Agnes overhears her children talking about putting the old family dog to sleep and panics when she assumes they are talking about her—something you could totally see happening in a chaotic, large Irish family household. Like Doyle, O'Carroll is a master at writing Irish dialogue.

For anyone who wants a taste of this comedy, just put Agnes Browne on YouTube; you will see snippets from the shows and plays that O'Carroll has staged with the Agnes character over the years. Of course, nothing beats reading a book—but I am preaching to the choir if you're reading this!

Larry Kirwan, *Green Suede Shoes* and *Liverpool Fantasy:* Kirwan's songwriting with Black 47 first drew me to him; the *Home of the Brave* album rocked just enough to make me pay attention to the Irish melodies that I swore I'd never like because they were jammed down my throat for so many years. When I heard the block-rockin' beats of "It's Time to Go" and "The Big Fellah," it was like getting an Irish history lesson from Public Enemy's Chuck D. I was hooked.

Kirwan branched out into plays and books, all of which have considerable artistic merit. His *Liverpool Fantasy* is a tale of an alternative universe that has the Beatles breaking up after their second single and reuniting a few decades later. A wildly inventive story, it falls just short of the rock 'n' roll autobiography *Green Suede Shoes*. *Shoes* is like *Angela's Ashes* and *Almost Famous* rolled into one. Yes, it's that good, and it is required reading.

W.B. Yeats, *The Collected Works*: Of course, reading Yeats during high school poetry classes was pure torture, but I have grown to respect the man madly in my later years.

When you write a novel, you can waste all the words you want if you can keep the reader's attention and deliver something worthwhile at the end of your tale. For poets, every word is measured against the rhythm; not a word gets wasted and each one must deliver a roundhouse punch. I could never write poetry, though I tried (see the "Screw U Haiku" chapter), and my hat goes off to writers in this genre.

His scalding desire for the young Maude Gonne in poems like "A Man of Young and Old" is a study in written desire: "My arms are like the twisted thorn/And yet there beauty lay/The first of all the tribe lay there/And did such pleasure take." Visiting his summer home Thoor Baylee, nestled in the verdant hills of County Galway, was a defining moment in my writing life. I am not one to subscribe to spirits communicating across the airwaves, but you can hear his whisper in the babbling brook that snakes around that castle. One of the most magical places on the planet, you must check your pulse if you fail to find inspiration here!

Cormac MacConnell, *Cormac's Corner* and *The West's Awake*: My esteemed colleague at *The Irish Voice* and IrishCentral.com is perhaps the most significant influencer on this little book you are holding in your hands and the one before that.

I became obsessed by the notion of starting and ending a story within one newspaper page the way he so effortlessly did in the pages of *The Irish Voice*. His storytelling became the watermark by which I measured my success. There were times that my father would call me once the paper came out and say, "I think you beat the auld fella this week," and that made my day because of how much my dad (and his mother before him) respected the man's mad writing skills. But most of the time, Cormac had me beat!

Cormac put out a compendium of his homespun stories from the west coast of Ireland. Cormac hears a story from his barstool perch about a heroic Irish cat that gets shot when he hops the fence and impregnates the pristine orange feline bloodline in a British estate in the North, the wheels turn, notes are jotted on a bar napkin, and a brilliant story is told to the readers the following week. I have seen him do this with my own eyes when I drank with him at The Honk, his beloved pub on the lip of Shannon Airport.

When he describes the sun tapping the rocks on the Cliffs of Moher "like golden slippers," you are transported to that magical land that tugs at our heart from 3,000 miles away.

Bruce Springsteen's albums (take your pick): You couldn't have grown up as a writer in New Jersey during a certain age and avoided his influence on your own writing. By the way, he is Irish-American and belongs on this list!

Yes, he is a wielder of power chords, but the magic can be found in the poetic lyrics. Take this example from "I'll Work for Your Love" from the *Magic* album. "Pour me a drink Theresa in one of those glasses you dust off/And I watch the bones in your back like the Stations of the Cross." It tells you everything you want to know about where the main character is sitting and the ache that he is stewing in, all in two lines. Novelists might spend a whole page getting the same point across, but not Bruce. There's not a word wasted for the sake of the rhythm.

His songs made people from New Jersey want to bust out of this place, and it made Jersey cool for the rest of the world. Amazing.

Book 4: Scribbling about Writing

Wait. Wait. WAIT! Before you turn the page because you don't think this section applies to you, I'd ask that you reconsider. Yes, the following few essays delve into the writing process, but there are also some life lessons in here as well. I talk about getting out of one's way and getting in touch with your own self-expression, things that might come in handy down the road when you pursue whatever your destiny might be. Promise.

Besides, I read somewhere that upwards of 87% of all people have either thought about writing a book or have a good book in them. You're not gonna bullshit me and say you're not one of them, are you? Read on.

How it All Began

Note: I wrote this piece for the commemorative 25th anniversary issue of The Irish Voice.

Do you have moments in your life when a seismic shift occurs and you can remember the exact time and place when it all went down? Allow me to share with you one of mine.

This particular Friday found me riding down to the hospital lobby in this elevator feeling pretty good about myself because within my briefcase was an order for nearly a half million dollars' worth of laboratory equipment. I was so lost in my own thoughts about how I was going to celebrate my win that I almost passed the gift shop; I backtracked a bit and went in to complete my weekly ritual of buying my copy of *The Irish Voice* there.

My custom was to flip first to the Off the Record column to get the latest news on the burgeoning New York rock scene. There it was on the page: a help wanted sign. The editors had posted it to replace the great Don Meade, who was moving onward and upward. I don't remember the turnpike whizzing by me after that because I had caught a fever of purpose and determination while at the hospital.

Looking back, I don't know what possessed me to apply. I had no journalistic experience whatsoever, except for a few pieces in my college newspaper 10 years prior. Nevertheless, I went to work as soon as I got home and put together thoughts on my favorite rock albums made by Irish or Irish-Americans.

Like a schoolboy cramming for a final, I meticulously assembled this faux portfolio to trick the editors into thinking that I had some great literary career. Fake it until you make it, I always say! Then I got the shock of my life: I was so immersed and excited in the prospect of becoming a writer for this paper that I completely forgot to place the equipment order in my briefcase!

That was the moment for me. When a career-making order that large failed to light you up, it was a telltale sign that you needed to make some changes. On the surface, I was leading a life full of consistent wins: a brand-new baby daughter, a career on the right trajectory, and a loving marriage. Yet even the great champions always look at the video playbacks of their games to see what's missing in their game, even when they win, so that they can bring a bigger game to the court next time. I had never done that introspection but knew innately that there was more to life than this and had just chalked it up to a pre-midlife crisis.

It was clear to me when I forgot to place that order what was missing in my game: creativity and self-expression. I had that sorted out and didn't care what the position paid, I thought. I would become the next Off the Record writer!

A few agonizing weeks later, the call came from editor Debbie McGoldrick: would I want to take a crack at a 500-700 word article on something? The audition had begun.

As luck would have it, I was going to Ireland the following week and had agreed to pop into a pub and have a look-see at the music scene over there. That one column turned into a series of half-page columns and then—Bob's yer uncle—I took over the whole page!

It's hard to believe this all went down 15 years ago.

Oh, and what adventures I've had and what things I've seen ever since! Press junkets to Ireland. Backstage pints with my heroes who had now become good friends. Eyeball to eyeball chats with the greatest musicians in our culture. Forceful eviction from Sinead O'Connor's penthouse hotel suite after she became enraged at a question I asked her. The endless parade of St. Patrick's seasonal activities. Front-row seats to U2 shows (until their management nixed that when I dared say one critical word about a crappy series of songs on one of their albums—"eff you" if you can't handle the truth!).The visits to the Irish Consulate. The governor's parties to honor the great Gerry Adams and Martin McGuinness. The list goes on.

The greatest adventure, however, has been the one within. There's this saying that God invented whiskey to keep the Irish from ruling the world, but I think there's a deeper reason for that. It's embedded in our culture to have a preoccupation toward what the neighbors think. "We'll be the laughingstocks at church," said my mother and many Irish mothers like her over the years; the possibility of that feeling is worse than death in our culture. To avoid that, we are taught to operate in narrow lanes, keep your head down, don't draw attention to yourself, and by all means, avoid doing or saying anything controversial.

I broke every one of those rules in the first four columns I filed for the newspaper and haven't looked back at that dull and boring way of being ever since. The check I got for those first four columns validated me as a writer—someone was now paying for those words! I never would have had the confidence in the way I slung ink on the page and I wouldn't have the writing life I have now if it hadn't been for Debbie McGoldrick and Niall O'Dowd taking a chance on this unknown Irish voice and I can never repay them for changing my life.

That first check also gave me a dose of reality that writing doesn't pay and few scribblers ever quit their day jobs. I'm still in the business of collecting large equipment orders at hospitals but now I have a team of people visiting hospitals. My million-dollar quota now sits at $200 million as a vice president of sales and I am clear that my rapid rise in the healthcare industry would not have been possible without injecting that creative outlet into my game of life.

The weekly writing discipline required to assemble Off the Record each week eventually led to the publishing of two books, and now this one.

Fifteen years on, I am immersed in the best year of my writing life. The musicians and publicists I've worked with all these years rolled up their sleeves when I asked them to and helped me drive "rock 'n' read" book signings for *This Is Your Brain on Shamrock*s. Many of the readers from the Off the Record column were kind enough to make themselves known along the way and have said very nice things about my work at *The Irish Voice* over the years. Plenty have also called me a right bollix for how misguided I am in my musical tastes and opinions, but bought a book anyway and I tip my hat to them as well!

So, with 15 years of *Irish Voice* pages in the rearview mirror, where do we go from here? Artists' interviews over a pint are giving way to more impersonal e-mail exchanges and Skyping, CDs in the mail have been replaced by website links and encrypted digital files, pub concerts and industry-only showcases are as rare as hen's teeth as artists stage YouTube shows instead. I've been saying, "I'm too old for this crap" each March 18 as I nurse a hangover and contemplate the prospect of another year of rocking and reporting. Who knows how long I can keep this up? And it must be said that the onslaught of online journalism and a tight economic climate with no foreseeable end has claimed many a newspaper (hence the explosion of our IrishCentral.com web portal).

During these uncertain times, I am reminded of an old Irish proverb: "time is a great storyteller." Whatever the future holds, I look forward to milking some good yarns out of it; don't be looking for a "help wanted" advertisement in the Off the Record column anytime soon!

A Write Pain

I'm sure the folks at the Irish-American Writers and Artists will revoke my membership card for saying it, but here goes: there's nothing more tedious than hanging out with other writers. Sad to say, some of the Irish ones are the worst.

I was at a book signing of a young and promising Dublin writer, and a wine and cheese event had suddenly broken out in the lobby. I gravitated toward the literati that I have come to know in this book-signing circuit. This little club is populated by writers feeling sorry for other writers because very few readers come to book signings and we don't want our book launch to look like Eleanor Rigby's funeral Mass.

"I finally came to grips with the fact that it's actually okay for me to pursue commercial success," said one natty writer as he swilled his wine and bit a slice of cheese with his butterscotch teeth. "Now I'm just trying to decide if I stick to my provocative novels and plays, run to these commercial pursuits, or bifurcate betwixt and between. What do you think?"

Well, you asked. You use "bifurcate" in a sentence and expect me to know what the hell that means? I faked an incoming text, excused myself, logged onto the dictionary app on my iPhone, and found that "bi·fur·cate" is a verb that means divide or fork into two branches. *Why didn't you just say so?* He prattled on and on about character development and before long, a rumpled vagabond revered in this circle of scribblers for writing brilliant plays that no one has seen began to nod knowingly. This just encouraged my bespectacled companion.

"Who wants to chase that road?" he asked with a sneer. "You pour your heart out on some book for 10 years of your life and then you're expected to go to a Costco warehouse aisle where the books are sold and some fecker might ask you where the Dubliner cheese is located. No thanks."

After about ten minutes of my listening to him, he asked, "What's the writing process like for you?"

"Well, it's like this," says I. "I address the bartender, order a whiskey, and have a seat. I tell stories. People laugh. I take notes. I fine-tune the story and on the next night, I order a whiskey. Rinse. Lather. Repeat."

"That's all?"

"Oh, yeah. I listen to people. A lot. I observe. I find something funny. Like tomorrow, I'm going to go back and make something funny out of this guy that used 'bifurcate' in a sentence with a straight face."

Nervous, skittish laughter ensued and the rumpled man did little to hide his contempt beneath the sunglasses he chose to wear in this darkened old church hall. They made small talk and backed away from the wine as quick as humanly possible.

Jhumpa Lahiri, author of *Unaccustomed Earth,* wrote a piece in the *New York Times* about the writing process. "As a book or story nears completion, I grow acutely, obsessively conscious of each sentence in the text. They enter into the blood. They seem to replace it, for a while. When something is in proofs I sit in solitary confinement with them. Each is confronted, inspected, turned inside out. Each is sentenced, literally, to be part of the text, or not. Such close scrutiny can lead to blindness. At times—and these times terrify—they cease to make sense."

I guess I just don't understand that tortured writer thing. I do understand ice cream, and I love the Ben & Jerry's motto: "If it's not fun, why do it?"

I usually go to my room and I look at writing as adult playtime.

I know you probably think it's impossible to conceive of an Irish man judging another man on how he does things, but I can't help but think that some people might be overthinking this writing business a wee bit. For those who say they want to scribble but have not, they usually make more of the writing process than there really is.

Maybe I'm the one doing it wrong? I see writers as a creative spirit free to choose heartache or happiness. Sure, even during funny moments in my writing you can see the pain, and many comedians harvest their best comedy from unpleasant chapters in their life. It's not like I have a pain-free life. But I choose to make humor out of it and find the funny side of it. I think there's nothing more grating than a fellow writer who blathers on about the torture he is putting himself through to complete a book that very few people ever read. If you are blessed to see a book through to its completion, be grateful!

If there's anything worse than getting all significant with writers writing things that no one has read, it's being in the presence of a gifted scribe whom *everyone* has read.

In New York Irish writing circles, the world spins around *Let the Great World Spin* author Colum McCann. The Dublin-born novelist has everything that the rest of us envy: he is the darling of *The New York Times Book Review*, he writes lyrics for rockers, has high-profile teaching engagements, is a fantastic cocktail-party conversationalist, and has two Man Booker prizes. Plus, he has just enough of a neck so that his artisan scarf drapes rakishly around it and he looks fantastic in tweed. Whereas I have no neck, my pale double chin nestles into a green scarf like an Easter egg on a pillow of plastic grass, and people have been known to get dizzy watching the vast expanse of patterns when I drape tweed over my significant stomach. Just when the new writers start to work the room, McCann saunters in and all the oxygen in the place follows his every step.

The whole room swoons over McCann, including the missus. "I'd shag him senseless," she growls under her breath after our pleasantries conclude and he turns his attention to another couple.

With that, I turn to her and ask her to say more about that, and a new column emerges. Some people think the greatest writing asset is having a way with words and some think it has everything to do with grammar and syntax. If you're having a hard time writing, shut up and listen—to your heart and to those around you. One voice I don't pay much attention to is the one inside my head that tells me what I am writing is *shite*. I say, "Thanks for your opinion" and keep writing.

So, think of this little essay next time you find yourself bifurcating between finishing that next novel and writer's block.

Write On!

So, is writing that book you always wanted to write on your list of New Year's resolutions? I say, go for it! My book tour made 2011 the best year of my life!

I shook a lot of hands and kissed a lot of babies campaigning for the first installment of *This Is Your Brain on Shamrocks*, and came across a lot of people with unfulfilled writing dreams.

"I always wanted to write a book," they would sigh. "But I could never get that done."

I remember the last time I said that. As a cub reporter for *The Irish Voice* a number of years ago, I found myself on the breezy porch of Mary Higgins Clark's Jersey Shore house. She had just written *Kitchen Privileges*, a short autobiographical story that she wrote for her grandchildren until her publisher snatched it away for public domain.

I had just gone through a litany of reasons and considerations on why I couldn't write: the toddlers always in diapers, the freakish travel, hectic meeting schedules, yadda, yadda, and more yadda. She sipped demurely from her dainty Belleek teacup, nodding occasionally. When I asked how she pulled a book each year out of thin air, she leaned in and gazed intently with those milky blue eyes.

"Y'know, there's a difference between me and you. I wanted it worse than you did. The best place to start a writing career is to shut up and start writing. There's no magic here."

When one of the top selling authors on the planet tells you to shut up and write, well, you shut up and write!

It was the best advice I had ever gotten before or since because I had a book outline within nine months of our interview, and a published novel within 18 months.

So, dear reader, my first advice to you is to shut up and write. Don't worry about whether or not it's good enough that someone might buy it. That stops most people from even picking up a pen and that's just a copout.

There are plenty of self-publishers out there that will happily load the book into BN.com and Amazon for you, which means your book can be e-reader ready without any need for an agent or big book company marketing arm, thank you very much. Who the hell are they to judge and assess your words?

And speaking of big book companies: if there's anything I heard on the book tour more often than "Gee, I always wanted to write a book," it was, "I never saw a dime after that crappy little advance check and I am convinced that my book company is screwing me over."

So, as the Irish say, all mountains look green from far away. I've run into dozens of famous writers out there crying in their beer and complaining about their book contracts. Think about that next time you waste a decade of the rosary moaning to the Lord about the rejection letters from would-be agents and publishers that hit your mailbox on a daily basis.

I got every royalty check that was owed to me, on a quarterly basis, no less—from my self-publisher. Scoff all you want about selling your book out of the trunk of the car: you make more per book that way and you know where every dollar goes. You maintain complete creative control over how the cover looks and how it gets into the right audience's hands.

I always cite Prince as a model of how to market your own art. He got so fed up by his restrictive record contract that he wrote the word "slave" on his face and submitted one crappy album after another to spite Warner Brothers. Once he was released from his contract, he began marketing directly to his fan base, making up to $5 more per unit sold when he rang the register, and created art on his terms. Not many people looked down their nose at him for being "self published" when he took to the Super Bowl halftime show stage in high heels a decade later. I rest my case.

The creative process doesn't just include writing the book, which is another common myth. You have to be a Mick Jagger type of artist: make a product that rocks, make a spectacle out of yourself as you promote it, and always have an eye on the bottom line. All at once.

Many of the snobby writers in the social circle I run in (this includes most of them) think the selling of art is beneath them. But I am of the belief that the marketing process is an extension of my self-expression. Using a combination of print media, websites, Facebook, Twitter, e-book signings posted on YouTube, and free excerpts placed on appropriate newsletters are the tools to build buzz about the book. For the first book in this series, as an example, I enlisted the help of some musician friends and we staged "rock 'n' read" events that enabled us to draw new sales from fans of one another's works. I'll probably do the same thing for the book you're reading now!

A well-executed launch strategy doesn't have to be a chore, nor does it have to be a commercial concern and sellout that is beneath your creativity. Let it be an extension of your creativity!

We would like to think that the whole world is waiting for our first book and that once we write it, we will be set for life. I'm sorry to tell you that neither one of these aphorisms is true. People are so fixated on their smartphones that many folks are contracting a "text message attention span" when it comes to reading. You literally have to compete with an iPad and a Facebook post for the entertainment mindshare of a consumer nowadays, something that never concerned Hemingway or Twain. Short blogs and essays increase the chances of the actual book being read. At least that's *my* experience—more people read my last book of essays than my 382-page suspense novel.

Murder mysteries are among my favorite things to read, but they are tricky for a new novelist. They look at the idea of writing volumes of fact or fiction and then get completely stopped and overwhelmed in their creative pursuits. Try writing little essays first and see what happens! You can either stitch the essays together into a larger plotline, see where the mind takes you in the writing process to unconceal a plotline that you wouldn't have otherwise thought of, or perhaps end up publishing a book of essays. I began writing essays years ago as an exercise in breaking a long streak of writer's block. They amused me, people liked reading them in the Irish press, and now we have two volumes of *This Is Your Brain on Shamrocks* in the can.

One more sore point before I get to the good stuff: I read somewhere that less than 150 novelists are walking around America slinging ink as their primary source of income. Many self-published books sell about the same amount of books as there are family members and Facebook friends, so you can do your own personal math. Some folks like me are lucky enough to get some national and international press, but even that only brings in a couple of thousand more than the average bear. If your book turns $5,000 in profit, consider yourself in the 1% of an "Occupy Bookshelves" movement. So, don't quit yer day job, laddies and lassies!

Are you discouraged yet? That wasn't my intent—quite the opposite. My writing life has made my life rich and delicious beyond my dreams and beyond any measure. While there are very few zeroes in my royalty checks, I have almost tripled my income in my chosen profession of medical device sales during a decade that has seen that industry shed jobs by the thousands.

The funny thing about being fully self expressed 24/7 is that your creativity is off the charts and your poor boss has trouble finding things to keep you challenged. They throw anything and everything at your insatiable creative engine just to feed it. You find yourself getting immersed in fun projects that give you a corner-office perspective and in a blink, you begin to think and act like someone who has a corner office, and then *voila!* You find yourself with a vice presidential title and are bestowed your very own corner office.

I remember moaning to Mary Higgins Clark about how little time I had to write. Now, I never complain about how busy I am because writing fulfills me and most of what life throws me doesn't seem so burdensome. Now that I just shut up and write, I find I have more time on my hands. That has allowed me to pursue my master's degree, learn bass guitar, start a web business venture, write a weekly column for *The Irish Voice*, consult for businesses on sales-force effectiveness, coach people on their effectiveness and power through Landmark Education, and write at a quicker pace since I began working on my first book.

So, let's review, shall we? If this is your year to write it all down, you need to be prepared for some things:

Be prepared for lonely nights at a monitor, getting more frustrated each time the cursor blinks.

Be prepared to laugh and cry at the monitor so much that you fear the day will come when the monitor writes a tell-all book of its own.

Be prepared to not have a lot to show in the bank account.

Be prepared to have other riches show up in your life.

Be prepared to play big or go home.

Be prepared to shut up and write.

Write on!

The Bonus Book

Fifty Shades o' Green: The Short Story

Ryan Logan parked his Volvo convertible next to the metered curb on the busy thoroughfare of McLean Avenue, fed the meter, and ambled into The Prodigal Son pub. The sun was still strong after dinner and his eyes had to adjust to the inky lowlights once he stepped inside.

He approached the sticky, lacquered bar and sat at the stool next to Johnny Rabbitte, his brother-in-law. He briefly put his arm around Johnny's bony shoulders as Johnny, on his cell phone, nodded and smiled. As he spoke, his hand combed his unkempt reddish hair beginning to streak gray.

"Howyis?" Mickey the jaundiced, blue-eyed bartender asked, wiping a bead of sweat captured in his woolly eyebrows. "A pint?"

"I'll have a pint," replied Ryan. He loosened his pink patterned tie. "No dinner in my house tonight, so make a burger with Swiss and mushrooms up for me, willya? My lady friend next to me will have herself a cosmo."

Johnny flicked his middle finger as Mickey fussed with the beer taps. Mickey moved with the nervous energy of an ant colony on a melting Popsicle.

"What brings yis in on a Monday night?"

"It's book club night at my house," replied Johnny, placing his iPhone on the bar. "So Ryan and I decided to start a liver-abuse club tonight."

"I'll drink to that," Ryan said, his eyes squinting at the television above the bar to catch the Mets.

"Jaysis, those book clubs are deadly altogether," said Mickey, the saliva mixing with the Nicorette gum he constantly chewed to create a yellow paste that emerged occasionally out of the side of his mouth. "Always readin' those chick-lit books. Putting all those romantic notions in their heads. They're not reading that Nicholas Sparks eejit, are they?"

"I don't think so," said Ryan.

"He's a right bollix altogether," said Mickey, his Cavan accent thickening as his story built steam. "Settin' this romantic standard that we all have to live up to. Like the other day I was walkin' with Mary 'round the neighborhood and we saw yer man next door kissin' his wife on the front lawn. Mary says, 'why don't ye do that?' Says I, 'Jaysis, I hardly know the woman!'"

"Not that joke again," groaned Ryan with an eye roll. "You can do better than that."

"Tonight they're reading that book *Fifty Shades of Grey,*" said Johnny tentatively, wiping his glass. "It's pretty hot stuff. Have your wives read it yet?"

"I saw it on the nightstand all right," replied Mickey, whose eyes manically jumped between the seventh inning on the screen and Johnny's face. "What's it about?"

"They're all talking about it on the morning shows," said Ryan as he fired off a text on his Blackberry. "They call it 'mommy porn.' I think there's bondage in it and that sort of stuff, right?"

"Ah, sure, that's nothin' new," Mickey said dismissively. "Me an' Mary's been doin' that S&M stuff for years."

"Really?" Ryan said, incredulity creeping into his voice.

"Yeah. She sleeps, I masturbate!"

They all roared. Mickey slammed his palm on the side of the bar.

"Did yis like that?" he shouted in between fits of laughter.

"That woman can write all she wants," said Johnny with a sly smile. "She'll get no complaints from me."

Ryan leaned in. "Is that right?"

"I haven't read the book, but there's apparently some pretty racy stuff in it," replied Johnny. "Lisa reads a chapter and then attacks me when we get to bed. It's been like we're on a second honeymoon or something."

"The book would be wasted in my house," Ryan sighed. "Sheila's in the home stretch of this pregnancy. She was good to go in the second trimester but that window has closed now."

"Did I ever tell you how much I love hearing about my little sister's sex life?" Johnny said with a grimace.

"Tough," replied Ryan, clinking his glass with Johnny's.

Johnny took a swig. "Anyway, you guys might want to have your ladies crack open that book," he said. "And brace yourself for a wild ride. My wife is into trying new things and everything. It's great!"

"Like what things?" Mickey lifted his elbows onto the bar.

Johnny looked both ways, his eyelids twitching, and Ryan rolled his eyes.

"Jesus! That drink didn't take long to do its work, Missus Lightweight."

"I'm fine," Johnny shot back.

Mickey swatted Ryan's shoulder.

"Will yeh let the man talk? What kindsa things?"

"Well, it started out that she just wanted it a bit more often," Johnny replied, licking foam from his lip. "We might have been down to once a week with the two little ones running around now. You know the drill."

"Sure, I know it well," said Mickey with an exaggerated head shake. "I'm down to once a month meself. Any longer in between shags and I'm gonna turn Franciscan friar."

Ryan shook his head and smiled. Mickey continued his interrogation.

"So, that was all? Just doin' it like mad, eh?"

"No, there's more. One night she came to the bed with a razor, shaving cream, and a bowl of hot water."
"Jaysis! Yer jokin'."

A broad smile broke across Johnny's face.

"I asked her what she was going to do with that. She took off her robe and I saw she was shaved clean!"

"I always thought Lisa was cute," said Ryan, cocking an eyebrow. "Now, I think I'm starting to fall in love!"

"Did she shave more of it?" The blood vessels rose in his face.

Johnny leaned into the bar.

"She shaved me," he whispered.

"Ah, g'wan. That must've hurt somethin' fierce, like."

"I'm serious! It was one of the hottest things that I ever had done to me," replied Johnny.

"Balls too?" Ryan asked.

Johnny smiled.

"Ah, now that was the best part."

"Where did she get such a ridiculous idea?" asked Mickey indignantly.

"That book, I guess. Plus, we'd been watching some videos."

"An' they're doin' that in dem videos?" asked Mickey.

"No! The actors are always shaved down there," Johnny replied.

"Man, you're dense, Mick."

Ryan snorted. "So, you're a porn star now? First Irish porn star...I could see the headline in the *Irish Voice* now."

"You can make fun all you want," Jimmy said, slurring slightly. "When Lisa hit chapter 8 of that book, my marriage changed forever. You should try it! The way you and my sister bicker , I think a little adventure in the bedroom would do you both some good."

Ryan's back stiffened.

"Yeah, we'll just fuck it out. That will solve everything. Whatever."

"Try it and find out," said Johnny with a simple smile. He took a sip of his beer, swirled it around his mouth, and raised his eyebrows before swallowing and moving his tongue through his teeth. He let some of his beer dribble down his chin before wiping it off.

"When's the last time that happened?"

Ryan flushed angrily. "A blowjob, you mean? Oh, please. Might I remind you that it's your sister we're talking about here?"

"I don't think that's right," said Mickey.

"You're damn right. That's my sister!" Johnny said, starting to giggle and then to hoot loudly.

"I'm talkin' about the shavin', yeh bollix," Mickey shouted. "God put hair down there and I think it's a sin to shave it off. Besides, it sounds disgustin', like a chicken breast and a hot dog slappin' at each other."

Ryan waved his hand for flair.

"Well, in Jimmy's case, it's like a chicken breast and a cocktail weenie slapping at each other!"

"Good one," said Johnny, reluctantly raising his hand for a high-five. "You can kid all you want, but that book is golden."

Ryan grabbed a spoon and put it near his mouth like a microphone.

"When there's no one else in sight! In the crowded lonely night, well I wait so long, for my love vibration, and I'm dancing with myself."

"I bet Billy Idol over here is doin' a lot of that dancin' with himself lately, with his wife up the pole like that," Mickey said flatly.

Ryan laid two twenties on the bar.

"I'm gonna take loverboy over here home to that sex kitten of his while he's still sober enough to find the right slot. Stay outta trouble, Mickey."

The crowd dispersed around 11:30. Mickey locked the doors and dipped the last few glasses into the hot water before placing them on the drain board. He entered the small kitchen, made and wrapped a turkey club sandwich, and climbed the stairs to his apartment over the bar.

The rooms all smelled like lemon-scented wood polish no matter what hour of the day; Mary would sometimes throw open the windows to disperse the scent when it was too strong even for her. The pleasantly dry and warm summer breeze lazily licked the Irish lace curtains as it washed into the spacious room.

"Howyis?" Mickey called out. There was no answer. He could hear the faucet running in the bathroom, and his mind flashed back to Johnny's story about the razor and bowl of hot water. In the kitchen he shook the kettle to make sure there was water inside before placing it on the range, took two dinner plates and a small serving tray from the cupboard, and set the table. He opened the Styrofoam clamshell packaging and laid the bursting club sandwich on the table.

Mary came out of the bedroom, her hair in a towel. She wasn't wearing a bra and her large breasts perched upon a trim belly underneath her tight T-shirt, which announced the Philadelphia Eagles, her beloved hometown football team.

After all these years, Mary Finn, yer a right flippin' ride, Mickey thought.

"Dem Jets fans might slit yer throat with a T-shirt like tha'."

"I have a strong man to protect me," she said with a wink. "How was the night?"

"Fine. For a Monday, like," was his reply.

"You like my new sweatpants?" She twirled like a runway model.

"Irish lingerie. Love it."

Mary shrugged and smiled. She took two mugs from a cabinet, and anchored the string of a Barry's tea bag around each handle.

"Who came in tonight?" she asked.

"Some ballplayers, some ladies. They mixed it up a bit. Always interesting to watch. Ryan and Johnny were in tonight as well."

"How are they doin'?" she asked.

"Fine," Mickey replied, stirring his tea with one hand and reaching for a half sandwich with the other.

"I had meant to get over to Lisa's book club night tonight but the day ran away from me."

Mickey raised his eyebrow and smiled.

"Yer not reading that book that everyone's talking about, dat fifty shades of whatever-the-hell-that-fella's-name-is, are yeh?"

"His name is Grey and I read the first one and I am through most of the second one," said Mary in between bites of the sandwich.

"What did yeh think of it?"

"Not particularly well-written. The sex scenes are a bit weird. Not sure what all the fuss is about, to be honest with you."

Mickey raised an eyebrow as he moved the mug of tea away from his lips.

"What about the sex scenes? The lads said their wives were ravin' about them."

"I guess those wives don't have older girls like we have," said Mary. She took the towel from her head and threw it on the back of the chair. Her black curls were shaking off the weight of the water in her hair. "I keep thinking of our Fiona being caught up with this sick dominating guy and it leaves me a bit cold. I think if she brought that Grey guy around the house and you knew what he was doing to your little girl, you probably would beat the crap out of him."

"Yer right about that," Mickey said with a laugh. Mary's no-nonsense approach to things was just like his mother's and that's what first drew him to her.

"Still," he ventured, "yeh have to wonder what all these women are seeing in it. I was in Costco the other day and there was a whole feckin' pallet of 'em in the book section."

"I mean, it's not totally awful." Mary tilted her head and met his gaze as she brushed the crumbs from the table into a cup made with her other hand. "It's over there on the table if you want to take a look at it. I'm going to go to bed and finish my book."

Mickey watched his wife's butt as she headed to the bedroom, then stared at the book for a minute before picking it up and bringing it back to the kitchen table. He remembered Johnny talking about how his marriage changed after Chapter 8, so he flipped through the book. He mouthed the words silently as he read it, a habit the Dominican nuns tried to beat out of him back in school at home. He was deep into Chapter 12 when the building surges in his loins became persistent.

"Jaysis," he said, his eye furiously scanning over his bifocals. He licked his fingers before turning every other page.

An hour later, he put down the book and stripped to his boxer briefs on his way into the bedroom. He brushed his teeth in the bathroom, swished Listerine around his mouth for a few seconds to mask the Nicorette smell that Mary hated, and washed his face with warm water and a face towel. He looked at his own body in the mirror for an extra minute.

Mary was propped up on a pillow with a book in her hand as he slipped in between the sheets.

"Looks like you were pretty hooked," she said with a smile, but without looking directly at him.

"I didn't think the book was that badly written," he said. "There were parts that got my attention."

"Like what?" Now she turned to face him.

He could feel the blood rush to his face.

"Oh, this and that. 'Tis amazing, really, what gets people goin', isn't it?"

Mary threw back the covers. She slipped in between them and propped her head on her hand and bent elbow.

"Oh yeah? Was there anything that got you going?"

"There's only one way to find out," whispered Mickey.
She flicked off the lamp on the side table and shimmied toward him. He cuddled up behind her backbone and reached under her shirt.

"How's dat feelin'?" Mickey said huskily.

"It's the perfect pressure if you're trying to jump a battery with cables," she said calmly. "Try a little tenderness."

The covers rustled as she turned to face him, meeting his mouth hungrily. He reached for her breast again but she stopped him by grabbing his wrists forcefully and pinning him to the mattress. She climbed on top of him.

"Mother of God," he said with a sigh.

He was asleep within seven minutes and snoring within eleven. Mary kissed Mickey's forehead, reached for the lamp, and grabbed her book from the nightstand.

■■■

Mickey was awoken by the sounds and smell of sizzling eggs and frying meat. He slipped on his white T-shirt and boxer briefs as he shuffled towards the kitchen. He found Mary tossing the bacon and black pudding around a frying pan. A plate of fried eggs and tomatoes were steaming on the kitchen table next to another plate of thick buttered brown bread.

"Morning, lover boy."

"Jaysis, that was epic," he said with a smile, swatting her ass playfully before reaching for the teakettle. "Getting on top like dat was nice. Brilliant, actually. We should try that more often."

"Works for me," said Mary.

"Twas like ye owed me money."

Mary looked up from the frying pan and glared at him playfully. "Way to ruin a mood! You're lucky you're good in the sack—I might throw this in your face."

Mickey squinted and fanned the air in front of him with the morning paper.

"A bit hot in here, innit?"

"I got the guy coming in a bit later to replace the air-conditioning unit in that window," she replied as she brought the meat to the table and sat down. "I have to run out to the Home Depot to get some caulking and the weather-stripping to put around the unit after he installs the new one. They say mice can come into the tiniest crack and I think that's how that one we had last week got in."

"I can go there if you want."

"That's okay, I'm heading over there to get the dry cleaning anyway."

Mickey nodded. He grabbed a fork and knife and tore into his breakfast. Mary fingered the lip of her mug of tea and watched him until he looked up at her silent smile.

"Do you have any old ties you don't need anymore?" she purred.

"I could put some on the bed later. Ye goin' to Goodwill with them?"

Mary looked down at the floor at her left foot, which was tracing a figure eight on the floor in front of her.

"No. I was thinking I'd pick up some duct tape if it's on sale at the Home Depot. Maybe we can use that with the ties? Y'know, for later?"

Mickey's face reddened. He looked down at his breakfast.

"That'd be grand. Feckin' brilliant, actually.

ABOUT THE AUTHOR

Mike Farragher has been writing for The Irish Voice and IrishCentral.com since 1997. He lives in Monmouth County, New Jersey with his wife and two daughters. This is his third book.

Made in the USA
Charleston, SC
14 May 2014